Victim Awareness Workbook

by Jonathan Hussey and Jo Richardson

About the Authors

Jonathan Hussey is one of the most exciting innovators of interventions for rehabilitating offenders today. He holds a B.Sc. (Hons) in Psychology from Loughborough University and a B.A. (Hons) in Community Justice Studies from Portsmouth University, as well as being a fully qualified, experienced, and award winning Probation Officer. Jonathan has worked extensively in the Criminal Justice System, but has specialised in leading roles within the Probation Service and Youth Offending Services. Jonathan currently works as a consultant for the Probation Service, and has established a successful training company; Intervention Consultancy (www.reoffending.org.uk).

Jo Richardson joined the Probation Service in 2005, initially within the Employment, Training and Education team before working as a Probation Officer from 2006. She works within a generic team managing offenders who pose a medium or high risk of serious harm to the public, including those within medium and high security mental health facilities, and of an extensive age range from young adults to elderly offenders. She is also trained as an Aggression Replacement Training (ART) facilitator, delivering this to both male and female offenders. Both her roles within the Probation Service have involved a high level of multi-agency working, including increasing the awareness of other agencies to the role of the Probation Service. Jo holds a BA (Hons) Community Justice, Portsmouth.

Should you, or your organization, require training on the delivery of these workbooks, then please contact Jonathan Hussey and Jo Richardson at interventioninfo@ymail.com

Table of Contents

Preface

How do you address an individual who commits a crime with little, or no, awareness as to how their behaviour impacts negatively on others? Do we just tell them what they did was wrong? Or do we help the perpetrators of this crime come to an understanding themselves; to create either a progressive movement, or 'light bulb' moment, related to the harm they have caused? Surely, if we believe people can change, then the latter will facilitate a better sustained change in an offender's behaviour? Developing this form of self-awareness is what this workbook sets out to achieve.

The use of language

In the following pages, this workbook will refer to the *facilitator, practitioner* or *tutor*. These terms mean the individual *delivering exercises* to the other person. These terms are interchanged, depending on the context, but they all mean the same thing here.

In turn, the following terms will refer to the person at whom the exercise is directed: *client*, *participant* and *offender*. Again these terms are interchanged, depending on the context.

The purpose of this workbook

The purpose of this workbook is to give the facilitator of any exercise an *easy-to-follow structure* to work from - with the client - to help build a basic level of victim awareness and empathy.

In order to build victim awareness and empathy in the client, this workbook is specifically designed to help the client consider the *consequences* of their actions and the *impact* it has on others. To do this, the exercises seek to help the client build a conscious recognition of the impact their behaviour has on both their own life, and the lives of those around them. By doing so, the motivation to 'change' should build up within the client.

Of course, this workbook does not claim that by completing the exercises the client will definitely have an increased level of victim awareness and empathy. However, if the facilitator can get the client to see the 'person behind their crime', it will hopefully act as an additional barrier to future problematic or offending behaviour.

As with all cognitive behavioural work, the majority of the exercises here are designed to create ambivalence (see section one) within the offender regarding their view as to the impact of their problematic behaviour, or offending towards their victims.

Who this workbook is for and the target client base

This workbook can be used on a one-to-one basis or adapted for use with a small group. It should primarily be used by individuals who work with offenders, including professionals in the Probation and Prison Service; this is why much of the emphasis is placed on offending behaviour. However, other professionals within schools, and drug or alcohol agencies may also benefit from the information contained in this workbook.

The targeted clients should have, at the very least, a basic level of literacy and prove motivated to discuss their problematic behaviour. Those who fully deny their offences or problematic behaviour, who say, for example: "Nothing happened and I was not there!" should not be considered suitable for the exercises in this workbook. Should the client, at the very least, accept that something *did happen* then they can be considered suitable.

It is worth recognising here, that many offenders may deny all, or parts, of their behaviour. This is perfectly normal as many clients may use denial as a means of justifying, accepting, or coping with negative behaviour. Should you wish to learn more about addressing denial then look out for our separate workbook on this topic.

When considering working with offenders specifically, the exercises within this workbook are applicable to most offenders and offence types. However, there are examples where the facilitator will need to modify, edit, or simply leave out an exercise. Care must also be given to challenge 'inappropriate' answers, with enough time planned for each session to cover this. Inappropriate answers in this instance could be anything which indicates the offender is thinking of themselves as a victim. An example of this is when the client states a short term impact of their offence to be: 'I found it traumatic to spend a night in a police cell', as this indicates they are considering the impact only on themselves. Another manner in which an inappropriate answer may manifest itself is in blaming the victim. An example of this is when a client states something to the effect of 'he/she was up for it' or the client provides a comment which indicates a belief that the victim 'encouraged' them to commit the offence.

Always be prepared to challenge inappropriate answers as they arise and in a motivational style (see section one). So, with this in mind, compare the brief conversations below and consider how this plays out in a session:

Practitioner: Tell me how you feel about your victim.

Offender: They got everything they deserved.

Practitioner: Well, that's an inappropriate comment. No victim is 'asking for it'. You assaulted them, you caused harm. How can you say someone 'deserved' that?

Offender: They were being antagonistic, they knew what would happen if they wound me up.

Practitioner: Only you are in control of your actions. You let them wind you up.

Offender: You're as bad as everyone else, you can't be bothered to listen to what I have to say. I'm not doing this. [walks out]

Compared to…

Practitioner: Tell me how you feel about your victim.

Offender: They got everything they deserved.

Practitioner: I'm not sure I follow you. Please explain more to me what you mean by the victim deserving it.

Offender: They wouldn't let up. They knew what would happen if they wound me up.

Practitioner: So you're telling me that it's the victim's fault and that you 'had' to assault them? You had no choice in how you behaved.

Offender: Yes, exactly. Well, kind of - but it wasn't much choice.

Practitioner: So your victim was controlling you?

Offender: No! But I'd had a bad day and I didn't want to deal with that stuff.

Practitioner: Did the victim cause your bad day?

Offender: No.

Practitioner: So if can you agree with the statement that the victim didn't cause your bad day, which is what made you angry and you then resorted to aggression - can we look at whether, in that case, the victim actually 'deserved' to be assaulted?

Offender: I'd not looked at it like that before.

What this workbook covers

This workbook is divided into two main sections.

Section One

This section covers some of the basic theoretical knowledge needed by the facilitator to undertake the accompanying exercises. It covers: What is Cognitive Behavioural Therapy (CBT), The Cycle of Change, Motivational Interviewing, 'Thinking Errors' and learning styles. Following an exploration into what each element is, we will explain briefly, where possible, how to undertake each skill.

Note: Should the facilitator already know these skills, then they can simply begin the exercises.

Caution: Section one is primarily for the practitioner's reference and is not designed to be shared with the offender. In our experience, it is useful for the practitioner to have some background knowledge of victimology - particularly if an offender needs to be challenged as to the 'point' of the work being undertaken. As such, there may be times when it is appropriate to discuss elements contained within section one.

Section Two

Section two covers the workbook exercises themselves. Here we shall explain exercises that will help the client build up a basic level of victim awareness and empathy.

Exercises within the workbook are broadly grouped into the categories of 'self-awareness' or 'empathy building'. These groupings will aid the facilitator in choosing relevant exercises if the intention is not to complete the workbook as a course. In addition to this, a basic, user friendly questionnaire will also be offered to help the facilitator review any change.

Note: This questionnaire should ideally be undertaken at the start and end of 'treatment' with this specifically meaning when the exercises have been run sequentially.

As stated above, the exercises in section two are ideally to be used in sequence. However, where appropriate, the facilitator can use the exercises as standalone tasks depending on the assessed needs of the client.

When assessing the client's needs, the facilitator must use their professional judgement as to where the client resides in the cycle of change (see section one) *and then* decide which exercises are relevant.

Should the facilitator want to run the exercises as a form of 'programme', then we suggest the following sequence:

1. **The Questionnaire**: this will help the tutor gain an understanding of where the client is with regards to their thinking. When considering an offender's level of victim awareness and empathy it is important to recognise changes following an intervention, both to the offender and in aiding assessments. This workbook is no different. The questionnaire we offer is intentionally simplistic and will help the facilitator easily quantify any changes once all the exercises have been completed.

2. **The Cognitive Behavioural Triangle**: This helps the client understand the link between thinking, feeling and behaviour. *Self-awareness.*

3. **Perspective Taking**: These exercises help the client recognise that there are other ways to look at circumstances. *Empathy building.*

4. **Defining a victim**: This helps the client know what a victim is. After all, how can we address issues if we do not know what they are? *Empathy building.*

5. **Direct and Indirect Victims**: Helps the offender understand that there are two ways in which any one offence could impact on others, as well as debunking the concept of a 'victimless' crime. *Empathy building.*

6. **The Effects of Crime on Others**: Examines the way in which crime has an impact on other people. *Empathy building.*

7. **The Effects of Crime on the Offender and their Family**: Helps build up an internal level of remorse and shines a light on how the client's behaviour can impact on their close relatives. *Self-awareness.*

8. **Understanding the Ripple Effects of Crime**: Teaches the offender how one action corresponds to another. *Self-awareness.*

9. **Understanding How an Offence Impacts on the Area an Offender Lives In**: Many offenders overlook this, but this exercise helps the offender learn about how their local area is affected by their actions. *Self-awareness and empathy building.*

10. **The Deeper Understanding of Being a Victim**: Role play; this helps the offender internalise in a 'real life way' how their behaviour affects others. *Self-awareness.*

11. **The Letter**: Builds on the offender's internal level of remorse by getting them to translate their internal feelings onto paper. *Self-awareness and empathy building.*

12. **The What If?**: Builds consequential thinking in an offender. *Self-awareness.*

13. **Review of the Trigger Triangle**: This is a fitting way to conclude the sessions, by reviewing how thoughts impact on feelings and affect behaviour. *Self-awareness.*

14. **The Questionnaire again**: Reviews the progress a client has, or has not, made.

Delivering the Exercises

Prior to each exercise, the facilitator will see **Tutor Notes**. These will give step-by-step guidance on how to run each exercise. The facilitator should read the notes and follow them. The subsequent worksheets for the client follows the Tutor Notes.

Now, regardless of whether the exercises are being delivered as a single session, or as a sequential programme, they should always be completed with a simple verbal 'summing-up' of what was covered at the end of each exercise.

Tip: the facilitator should never start a session without thinking carefully about, and planning for, examples of answers that the offender may offer. It may sound obvious but if the facilitator is stumped by a question then the exercise can lose its intended impact. This also helps prepare the facilitator to address potentially inappropriate or anti-social answers.

Lastly, when undertaking any exercise, the facilitator should never be afraid to use a *neutral* example from their own lives as an illustration of the types of answers that the exercise is attempting to draw out from the client. However, these examples should **not** be deeply personal – these exercises are for the client, not therapy for the facilitator, nor to place the facilitator at risk.

Out of Session Work (optional)

Following each exercise, and to offer more to the client - thus reinforcing learning - optional out of session work is also suggested. These out of session work exercises can be used if the practitioner feels that it would be beneficial for the offender. However, it is not a required part of proceedings.

Adapting the Sessions and Alternative Exercises

Understanding a client's *learning style* (see section one) is imperative for ensuring that the client really understands what is being put to them by the tutor. Therefore, within this workbook, we also offer an alternative way to deliver each exercise where possible.

Section One

Cognitive Behavioural Therapy

This workbook uses the theoretical basis of Cognitive Behavioural Therapy (CBT). Cognitive behaviourism as a whole, and in relation to working with offenders, works towards achieving a sense of personal responsibility within the offender for their behaviour and the resultant consequences (Chui, 2003:68-9). So, if the facilitator can motivate the offender to take responsibility for their behaviour and consider the consequences of their negative actions, then the offender may change their negative behaviours accordingly. But how does CBT enable the facilitator to do this?

CBT in itself is a form of therapy which aims to create an 'ability' in the person to address their problems. Unlike other therapies, it is rooted in the 'now' and looks at how our emotions colour how we approach any given situation. It also helps the client to understand how previous experiences may have shaped our current values and behaviour.

Through CBT, an offender can come to understand their own motives better, and challenge their problematic behaviour; replacing it with more pro social actions. In basic terms, the CBT approach believes that by changing someone's thinking, especially 'flawed' thinking, the resultant behaviour will also change. So, in keeping with the CBT approach, within this workbook, the exercises we propose will help the client consider the implications of their actions by changing their thinking.

The Cycle of Change

The *Cycle of Change* was developed by DiClemente and Prochaska as an aid to assist people in understanding why some people are able to make (and sustain changes) whilst others fail to recognise the need for change. It is also a model that provides a foundation for understanding the stages an individual 'progresses through' when trying to change their behaviour.

The Cycle of Change very simply breaks down the process of change into six areas defined by a person's motivation, and indeed ability, to change (Hussey 2012). We believe that it is critical that the facilitator understands the concept of the Cycle Of Change because one of the aims of this workbook is to increase the client's internal level of motivation to change by, at the very least, moving them firmly into the *contemplation phase* of this cycle, if not through to the *preparation phase*. So, what are these phases?

Using an offender as an example again, initially, a person may begin in a stage called *pre contemplation*, where there is no recognition of an existing problem. With offenders, this can be seen as a state of denial related to either the offence or the harm it has caused.

Through creating ambivalence towards an offender's current lifestyle, movement can be made towards *contemplation* where a person begins to identify drawbacks to their choices and starts to desire change.

The next stages are *Preparation* (also known as *decision*) and *action*. *Preparation* to change and *action* are rather self-explanatory. These phases often occur in quick succession as the motivation brought about by a decision to change behaviour feeds into the actions to alter their behaviour in accordance with their newly desired decision(s). If progress through these stages is achieved, then the person can move forwards to *maintenance* (Fleet and Annison, 2003; Winstone and Hobbs, 2006:262-8).

Note: Should the client conclude in the decision phase that change is too difficult, or 'not worth the effort', this results in a return to a state of pre contemplation.

Assuming that the client is now in a stage of maintenance, there is some debate about the next movement of the client. This debate centres around whether, having made a change, a person remains in the maintenance phase permanently, or whether he/she leaves the cycle when that change becomes internalised or a 'habit'.

As stated in Hussey (2012), for some to remain in the cycle forever is a rather depressing thought and so to aim to practice and perfect a change, to the point where exiting the cycle in a positive manner is achievable, can be a more encouraging viewpoint.

As mentioned above, the potential to exit the cycle at any stage through a lapse or relapse to old behaviours is always possible. A 'lapse' tends to refer to a momentary slip to previous behaviours, which can subsequently lead to either a return to the cycle or an exit from the cycle via a 'relapse' and the abandonment of change (Winstone and Hobbs, 2006:262-8).

For the visual learners amongst you, here is a diagram of the Cycle of Change:

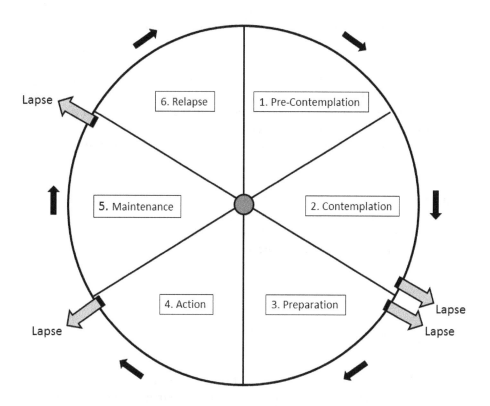

How to use the Cycle of Change

Using an offender who has just been sentenced as an example, and anticipating that the offender who undertakes the exercises is at the beginning of their sentence, we will assume that they are in the pre contemplation stage (with a belief that they do not need to change) regarding their offending behaviour. Here, the practitioner would use their understanding of the Cycle of Change to create ambivalence within the offender concerning offending - in an attempt to move them to the next stage of contemplation. To do this, the practitioner should try to create doubt in the client about the validity and worthwhileness of the offending behaviour. The facilitator should also try to encourage the offender to (at least) entertain the idea that there are other options. This stage can very much be the 'drip drip' approach to eroding seemingly set ideas.

Once an offender has moved into the contemplation stage, where they are open to discussing and even admitting that their offending behaviour is harmful, more work can be undertaken to underpin this theoretical shift; in particular the way the offender views the world towards more concrete behavioural choices and actions. This period can be a very unnerving time for the offender because they are, in many ways, 'undoing' what they thought they knew. So if this happens, and they start to move back to pre contemplation, the facilitator should do their best to support the offender in considering new options and moving them to the decision stage where there is a conscious choice to change.

Note: See how the above says 'assist' and 'support' not *advise*. Advice is a very thorny topic; no one generally wants to be told what to do and even when it is given, accepted and acted upon, then it will probably not be a lasting change as it *was not that person's choice*. The practitioner is there to help the offender make new decisions, not tell them what they should be doing (no matter how tempting this may be) under the guise of 'advice'.

Once the offender has decided to change and puts their new thoughts into action, it is here that the facilitator should discuss with them the obstacles of maintaining their new path. The reason for this is not to be negative or to encourage them to fail, but to allow them to realise and accept how it is going to be a difficult transition and that they should not just give up at the first hurdle, or indeed lapse.

The 'Ripple Effect'

The idea of the 'ripple effect' is used in several of the exercises in section two. It is the notion that whatever actions we do and whatever decisions we make, no matter how big or small, there are consequences and repercussions beyond what we may have expected for the original behaviour. There are several ways of visualising this; there is the classic 'butterfly flapping its wings in the amazon causing a typhoon in Japan', or more subtly, the rings of water reaching out to a pond's edge following a stone being dropped into the water. Another example might even be the tectonic movement of the Earth's plates – they move at the pace of fingernail growth but they still cause the formation of mountains. When discussing this idea with an offender, it needs to be applied so that they begin to understand that whilst they may consider their offence 'minor', the unintentional impacts above those directly involved can be immense. The aim is to remove a client's blinkers and increase self-awareness with regard to the community and society.

What are Cognitive Distortions ('thinking errors') and how can they be recognised?

In order to move offenders forward within the Cycle of Change, this workbook seeks to explore the impact and consequences of the client's behaviour (with the client) on the victim and the community and in doing so raise their awareness. It also explores the client's own feelings of being a victim in order to help them empathise with the victim of their offence.

10

Here, caution should always be exercised in order to prevent the client from building up cognitive distortions. But what are cognitive distortions?

In brief, a cognitive distortion is a 'thinking error' (Hussey 2012). It is a particular way of looking at a fact, or part of life, which acts to overemphasise or exaggerate that issue, often leaving no alternative or way back once identified as 'fact'. For example, an offender may have decided that 'all the Police' hate them and therefore be unable to consider approaching authority for assistance. The fact that very few people are 'always' targeted by Police, and that all Police Officers will differ in their approach towards their treatment of offenders, and that each meeting with the Police is likely to be a different experience is too much detail for the distortion and as such these facts are dismissed by the offender's thinking error.

Sometimes, a cognitive distortion can be a comfortable way of thinking for an offender (or anyone for that matter) even if it is incredibly negative and damaging, because there are no subtleties or unknowns. Therefore change is difficult.

Cognitive distortions do not always lead to offending behaviour and examples of distortions can be found in most aspects of life. However, where distortions related to offending are identified, they can be key in understanding both why an offender chooses to behave in such a manner, and also how to address that behaviour. Using the 'trigger triangle', covered later, cognitive distortions provide an illustration of the possible thoughts which are feeding an individual's offending behaviour.

Cognitive distortions are typically associated with depressive thinking and there are many different types of cognitive distortions. Discussion of these is beyond this workbook. Knowledge of them can be gained from further reading and practitioners may find such additional reading useful. Should you want to read more on the types of thinking errors then a useful book in exploring these is the related book (written by this one of this workbook's co-authors, Jonathan Hussey) entitled: *Reoffending: a practitioner's guide to addressing offending behaviour in the Criminal Justice System*.

A working example of a cognitive distortion from real life practice could be when an offender tells themselves: "I am a bad person" when, in fact, it is only part of their behaviour which is bad. They may, in fact, be a very pleasant person ninety-nine percent of the time and it is only one percent of the time when their behaviour can be seen as 'bad' or antisocial. This type of thinking error or cognitive distortion is called over-generalising. So, by highlighting the cognitive distortion to the offender, and breaking it down through exercises, the offender is given the opportunity to adjust their thinking and change their behaviour.

When considering the above, it is the internal dialogue which will enable an offender to move through the Cycle of Change and it is therefore envisaged that the practitioner will support victim awareness work with other offending behaviour work, as well as more holistic support, running concurrently.

What is Motivational Interviewing?

Motivational Interviewing (MI) is a method of working with offenders created by Miller and Rollnick (1991). Where other methods may build a relationship in which change can happen - MI provides a method of progressing and directing that change.

MI is a particular way of facilitating the recognition of problems and addressing them; motivation is a fluctuating state and MI uses a systematic strategy to build internal motivation to tackle these - rather than external pressure (Miller and Rollnick, 1991 cited in Fleet and Annison, 2003:133), linking it to normative compliance. Confrontation is an aim of, rather than a process of, MI (Winstone and Hobbs, 2006:259). However, it is important to note that this confrontation is not code for 'argument' with the offender. The confrontation regards their ideas and statements.

There are five key principles:

1. Being empathetic and accepting of the individual although not the behaviour
2. The development of discrepancies in an offender's cognitive distortions leading to the questioning of beliefs
3. The avoidance of argument through rolling with resistance
4. Seeing resistance as part of an offender's reaction to discomfort with the realisation of their cognitive distortions
5. Supporting efficacy through building belief in the offender's own abilities

(Fleet and Annison, 2003:133-6).

MI is often linked to the Cycle of Change as its principles can be integrated into the cycle. A substantial advantage to MI is that it can be delivered effectively in one session. MI also introduces protective factors which can be considered as reasons to sustain any changes made within a lifestyle. Ideally these protective factors would be internal beliefs rather than external, as the potential for an external factor to change or 'let down' the offender (if it were a person they were changing 'for', for example) can create the potential for lapse (Winstone and Hobbs, 2006:284). It is worth noting, however, that female offenders may pick an external factor such as their child and that this could be linked to social bond theory considerations such that family responsibilities are likely to cause desistance in female offenders (Rex, 1999:374).

As with any approach, there are no guarantees for success; an offender may exit the Cycle of Change by decision if they determine that they are content with their current lifestyle and the process of using MI would need to begin again.

How to do Motivational Interviewing

MI involves being able to direct a conversation with a person so that they are able to discover a truth for themselves. The practitioner needs to be able to read the feedback from the person sat with them in the form of both verbal and non-verbal communication. Listening to what the person is trying to say and reflecting this back to them, either to highlight a discrepancy with their statements or to enable them to find the meaning, are crucial skills. Unhelpful statements are those that contain advice, threats, criticism or direct commands - however tempting.

During any one session, several things are important; being specific in the feedback that is given to the offender (especially praise), listening carefully to the client, using both summarising and reflective listening to prove that the client has been heard, making sure questions are open questions, and encouraging self-motivating questions. These are all evidence that MI is in use.

If the offender resists or is disruptive then change the practice approach, do not attempt to force them to change.

An example discussion using MI:

Practitioner: Thank you for being punctual. I've noticed that you've been on time the last two sessions. Today we need to look again at your index offence.

Offender: Again? It's hardly important. They shouldn't have left their bag on the chair like that if they didn't want it taken.

Practitioner: So you think that it's the victim's fault for not safeguarding their possessions?

Offender: That's not what I said.

Practitioner: Explain to me what you meant?

Offender: It's just that I need to get money and sometimes if it's made easy for me to take something, then I will. They obviously didn't want it that much if they were willing to leave it lying around.

Practitioner: So you feel the victim wouldn't have had much of a reaction to finding that their bag and possessions had been taken?

Offender: Well, no. I don't know. I've not really thought about it.

Practitioner: Okay. Let's look at it now. Tell me how you think the victim may have reacted and what they may have felt.

Offender: I don't know. I'm not doing this, it's pointless.

Practitioner: No worries. Have you ever had anything taken or stolen from you?

Offender: Yes.

Practitioner: Tell me about that, and how you felt.

Offender: I had my Xbox nicked by a so-called mate. It made me really angry and I was kind of upset as I'd had to save for ages to get it.

Practitioner: That sounds pretty awful. Especially as it was something you'd worked hard for.

Offender: Yeah.

Practitioner: Thinking about the victim of your offence again, how do you think they may have felt?

Offender: Alright, alright. They might have felt angry and upset too.

What are learning styles? What are the factors to consider for each style?

We do not all learn in the same manner, and learning styles are a way of recognising this. There are three main recognised ways in which we learn:

Auditory: where preference is given to listening to relayed information through lectures or discussions.

Visual: where a person is best able to take in information they can 'see' in the form of presentations, books and diagrams.

Kinaesthetic: where learners prefer to 'do' in order to learn for themselves.

Evidence has shown that offenders tend to be kinaesthetic learners, requiring a participatory approach rather than a didactic one (Hopkinson and Rex, 2003:165) and this is worth bearing in mind when considering the manner in which to deliver an exercise, or whether it needs to be broken down over several sessions. There are various questionnaires available which can be completed with an offender to determine the best style of learning for them. However, caution should be exercised when labelling an offender as having a particular style. It is only a guide and not a necessity to subsequently present all information rigidly in that manner.

This workbook provides some examples of presenting the same exercise in different styles, however almost any exercise can be adapted. It doesn't have to be a complex process to change information from a diagram to spoken or as an 'experiment'. Below are three ways of presenting the same information regarding an offender's sentence:

Auditory Simply stating: "You were sentenced to three years in custody. You've now served half of that in prison and so been released. You will spend the rest of your sentence on licence. Part of that licence is to report weekly to Probation for supervision where we will undertake work to address issues related to your offending. If you fail to attend these appointments, or break any other conditions of release, such as committing another offence, then you may be recalled to prison."

Visual

Kinaesthetic Chop the above diagram into pieces and ask the offender to reassemble the diagram (like a jigsaw) with discussion as to why they think pieces go in certain places.

Victimology and the wider use of victim awareness (optional reading)

Interestingly, there is no one accepted definition of a victim (Tapley, 2007:9). Instead variations exist which are subject to current social norms and values. The majority of definitions find common consensus in that victims have been in receipt of harm, for example the United Nations definition: "persons who … have suffered harm, including … injury, emotional suffering … [or] loss." (UN, 1985 cited by Tapley, 2007:9) but this harm must result from an act which is illegal in the place where the act occurred.

The Probation Service's definition of a victim is 'an appropriate person' under the Criminal Justice and Court Services Act 2000, explained as 'any person in relation to an offence who appears … to be, or act for, the victim of the offence.' (PC05/2000:2). It is worth noting that the label of victim creates a homogenisation when risk and experiences of victimisation actually vary (Spalek, 2003217-8). It is also critical to bear in mind that victims and offenders are not separate populations (Farrell and Maltby, 2003:22).

There have been several Acts passed in recognition of victims: the 1964 creation of Criminal Injuries Compensation, reparation through Community Service and Compensation Orders as sentencing disposals in 1975 and 1982 respectively (Rock, 1990 cited in Tapley, 2007:35), followed by the Victims Charters' of 1990 and 1996 (Spalek, 2003:216) in which CJS agencies' duties towards victims were stated (however not until the Criminal Justice and Court Services Act 2000 were these duties made statutory). And more recently passed, the Domestic Violence, Crime and Victims Act 2004 and Legal Aid, Sentencing and Punishment of Offenders Act 2012.

Victimology began in the 1940's with the work of von Hentig and Mendlesohn. Both aimed to further understanding of the role of the victim in crime; von Hentig through victim proneness and Mendlesohn through victim culpability (Walklate, 2004:33). This was further extended by Wolfgang (1957) and Amir (1971) with theories of victim precipitation and more recently through concepts based on lifestyle risk factors (Hindelang *et al* (1978) cited in Walklate, 2004:34). These theories are essentially positivistic as they concern the identification of individual risk factors in victimisation.

The positivistic notion of an 'ideal' victim is worth having an understanding of - as an offender may use the flip side of this to minimise the harm of their offending. If their victim was not engaged in reasonable behaviour themselves at the time of the offence, for example. Indeed, an offender may use their experience of the Criminal Justice System to 'back up' this cognitive distortion. Whilst the idea of stereotypes in the CJS is an uncomfortable one, it has been identified before. Research by Gilchrist and Blissett (2002) found that Magistrates, when asked to explain their sentencing in domestic violence cases, used victim blaming statements similar to those used by defendants and were more likely to impose a Community Order compared to a similar assault on a stranger, where the sentence became custody. As far back as 1979, research has determined that cases where the victim had been engaged in misconduct prior to the offence led to less harsh punishments for the offender (Myers, 1979:534). However, if victim lifestyle choices are to be considered, then what about career choices such as probation officer, where the person chooses to work in a 'risky' environment? Are they then a less deserving victim if assaulted by an offender (Trulson, 2005:407-9)?

Increasing victim empathy as a method of reducing future offending is used to its greatest impact through Restorative Justice (RJ). Whilst this workbook does not guide the practitioner to work with the victim of an offence, its roots in the power of awareness of the consequences of offending behaviour, outside of the offender's 'world', are shared.

RJ ideally culminates in the meeting of the offender and their victim, where the victim is able to speak with and ask questions of the offender - and the offender themselves, in an ideal world, apologises. The idea is not a new one but is taken from various sources throughout history, including the Maori peoples in New Zealand. Most recently, RJ has had something of a renaissance as reoffending becomes a politically important topic. The Ministry of Justice Green Paper 'Breaking the Cycle: Effective Punishment, Rehabilitation and Sentencing of Offenders' (MoJ, 2010) covered the increased use of RJ within sentencing and as a diversion from the Criminal Justice System for lower level offending.

In its simplest form, RJ presents a literal translation of what this workbook is trying to achieve; it forces the offender to see the victim as a person with their own fear, concerns and impact resulting from the offence.

In relation to RJ and meeting the victim, there are limitations of appropriateness. Substantial consideration must be given as to whether a meeting of the victim and offender would constitute revictimisation of the victim. As such, some offence types are not considered suitable, for example domestic abuse or sexual abuse cases.

Increasing victim awareness is therefore not a new idea. However, this workbook aims to bring together ideas which have been used to great effect previously (as well as new initiatives) into one place, which the practitioner can then use as a programme of work or as a 'pick and mix' of exercises to deliver. Practitioners need to be careful to avoid delivering victim awareness as one 'lump' of work. 'Victim awareness' can be spoken of as a separate entity but its effectiveness relies on integration with other interventions. Arguably there are limits to empathy, especially where there is a cost involved to the giver. It tends to be empathy along with a moral 'code' that provides the motivation to change or act. It is the other interventions which assist in building this moral code and, together, all the interventions aim to assist the offender in wanting to be part of a law-abiding society.

Bibliography

Chui, W. H. (2003) What Works in Reducing Re-Offending: Principles and Programmes. In W. H. Chui and M. Nellis (Eds.) *Moving Probation Forwards: Evidence, Arguments and Practice*. pp56-70, Pearson Longman: Essex

Farrell S. and Maltby, S. (2003) The Victimisation of Probationers. *The Howard Journal,* 42(1), 32-54

Fleet, F. and Annison, J. (2003) In Support of Effectiveness: Facilitating Participation and Sustaining Change. In W. H. Chui and M. Nellis (Eds.) *Moving Probation Forwards: Evidence, Arguments and Practice*. pp129-143, Pearson Longman: Essex

Gilchrist, E. and Blissett, J. (2002) Magistrates' Attitudes to Domestic Violence and Sentencing Options. *The Howard Journal*, 41(4), 348-363

Hussey, J. (2012) *Reoffending: A practitioners Guide to Working With Offenders and Offending Behaviour in the Criminal Justice System*. Bennion Kearny: Birmingham

Ministry of Justice (2010) *Breaking the Cycle: Effective Punishment, Rehabilitation and Sentencing of Offenders.* HMSO: London

Myers, M.A. (1979) Offended parties and Official Reactions: Victims and the Sentencing of Criminal Defendants. *The Sociological Quarterly*, 20, 529-440

PC05/2005 (2005) *Investigation of Serious Crimes Involving Offenders Under Probation Supervision – MoU Between the Police and Probation Services relating to Victims.* National Probation Directorate: London

Rex, S. (1999) Desistance from Offending: Experiences of Probation, *The Howard Journal*, 38(4), 366-383

Spalek, B. (2003) Victim Work in the Probation Service: Perpetuating Notions of an Ideal Victim. In W.H. Chui and M. Nellis (Eds.) *Moving Probation Forwards. Evidence, Arguments and Practice*. pp.215-225 Pearson Longman: Harlow

Tapley, J. (2007) *Victimology: Victimisation and the Criminal Justice Response*. University of Portsmouth: Portsmouth

Trulson, C.R. (2005) Victims' Rights and Services: Eligibility, Exclusion, and Victim Worth. *Criminology and Public Policy*, 4(2), 399-414

Walklate, S. (2004) *Gender, Crime and Criminal Justice (2nd ed.)* Willan: Devon

Winstone, J. and Hobbs, S. (2006) *Strategies for Tackling Offending Behaviour, Volume 2*. 231-395, University of Portsmouth: Portsmouth

Section Two

The Questionnaire

Tutor Notes The questionnaire provided is designed to help the facilitator gain an understanding of *where* the client is with regards to their thinking. It is primarily aimed at those who have been convicted of a crime but it can be used in other circumstances where a problematic behaviour has occurred and which is admitted (at least partially) by the client. This questionnaire is to be used at the start, and end, of treatment.

Step 1: The facilitator asks the client to complete the questionnaire as honestly as possible.

Step 2: The facilitator totals up the 'score' and makes a note of it. Depending on the receptiveness of the client, this can be done during the session with them, or at a later time.

Step 3: Store the completed questionnaire safely and review it once the post programme questionnaire (the questionnaire at the end of this workbook) has been completed in order to evidence any positive changes in the client's victim awareness and empathy.

Note: It is, in some cases, a good idea to challenge any anti-social ideas which are evidenced through this questionnaire. However, this should occur in a separate session and without direct reference to the questionnaire itself. Challenging the answers given in this exercise directly may lead the offender to feel they are not able to answer honestly. Most offenders will 'know' what answer they 'should' give, but this will not aid a practitioner in assessing levels of victim awareness.

The Initial Questionnaire

Please circle the answer that best describes how you feel about your offence and explain further where required.

Answer on a scale of 1 to 5, where 5 is you agree strongly with the statement, and 1 is where you totally disagree.

1. I am the victim of my offence.

1   2   3   4   5

If you have circled 3 or above, please explain your answer here:

2. My offence has not affected anyone else.

1   2   3   4   5

If you have circled 3 or above, please explain your answer here:

3. The offence was the victim's fault.

1   2   3   4   5

If you have circled 3 or above, please explain your answer here:

4. I did not think about how my offence would impact on others before I acted.

1   2   3   4   5

If you have circled 3 or above, please explain your answer here:

5. My offence has not impacted on the victim's family.

1   2   3   4   5

If you have circled 3 or above, please explain your answer here:

6. My offence has not affected the community I live in.

1   2   3   4   5

If you have circled 3 or above, please explain your answer here:

7. Looking at the scale of offending in this country, my offence is relatively minor and unimportant.

1   2   3   4   5

If you have circled 3 or above, please explain your answer here:

8. There are other people involved in my offence who need to take some responsibility for my offending.

1   2   3   4   5

If you have circled 3 or above, please explain your answer here:

9. There is a lot of fuss being made about the victim, instead of considering my feelings.

1   2   3   4   5

If you have circled 3 or above, please explain your answer here:

```
┌─────────────────────────────────────────────────────────┐
│                                                           │
│                                                           │
│                                                           │
│                                                           │
│                                                           │
│                                                           │
└─────────────────────────────────────────────────────────┘
```

10. The consequences of my offence are limited to the short term.

1   2   3   4   5

If you have circled 3 or above, please explain your answer here:

```
┌─────────────────────────────────────────────────────────┐
│                                                           │
│                                                           │
│                                                           │
│                                                           │
│                                                           │
└─────────────────────────────────────────────────────────┘
```

11. Paedophiles who are murdered because of their offending behaviour are not victims.

1   2   3   4   5

If you have circled 3 or above, please explain your answer here:

```



```

12. If the victim had reacted differently once the offence had started, events may have been different at the end.

1   2   3   4   5

If you have circled 3 or above, please explain your answer here:

```



```

13. It is difficult to think about a 'victim' as a victim, when that victim is a large organisation, a shop or the community.

1   2   3   4   5

If you have circled 3 or above, please explain your answer here:

14. I agree that whilst my actual offence is illegal, in my circumstances there should be more understanding and less punishment.

1   2   3   4   5

If you have circled 3 or above, please explain your answer here:

15. There was no victim, only potential victims.

1   2   3   4   5

If you have circled 3 or above, please explain your answer here:

16. The cost to the community of offending, in terms of money or emotions, is minimal.

1   2   3   4   5

If you have circled 3 or above, please explain your answer here:

17. I believe victims should have to attend crime awareness courses so that they can prevent themselves from being victims again in the future.

1   2   3   4   5

If you have circled 3 or above, please explain your answer here:

```


```

18. This focus on victims and victim awareness is not going to help me.

1   2   3   4   5

If you have circled 3 or above, please explain your answer here:

```


```

19. There is only a 'long term' impact to my offending because professionals won't stop talking about the offence.

1   2   3   4   5

If you have circled 3 or above, please explain your answer here:

```



```

20. Even if I knew just before my offence/at the time of my offence, that my behaviour would create a victim, I do not think that I would have behaved any differently.

1   2   3   4   5

If you have circled 3 or above, please explain your answer here:

```



```

Please add up your scores and put the total here:

Thank you for completing this questionnaire.

The Exercises

You can adapt the exercises to all variations of problematic behaviour and which do not necessarily include offending behaviour.

Despite, our use of the term "offender", as discussed in section one of this workbook, this by no means excludes other problematic behaviours by the client which they freely admit too. For instance, this workbook is ideal as a form of intervention for a young person who has maliciously pushed another pupil at college (where police action has not been deemed necessary) or indeed instances of bullying.

The exercises have been written with a target audience of both male and female clients, aged fifteen and older. However, should a practitioner feel that a younger person would benefit from this workbook, care would need to be taken to ensure the language used and examples within exercises are appropriate.

At the end of any exercise, the facilitator should ask the client what they have learned from that exercise. The answer should then be written onto the worksheet. The reason for this is that once the facilitator has completed all the exercises they want to use with the client, the learning points (which are personal to the client) can be summarised and fed back to the client, in keeping with the MI style of working (see section one).

Exercise 1 – The My Trigger Triangle

Category of exercise: Self Awareness

Tutor Notes

The Cognitive Behavioural Therapy (CBT) Triangle is an important element which, for the purposes of this workbook, should be explored first by the tutor with the offender. So, to undertake this exercise, the tutor will need to know what the CBT Triangle is within the context of this workbook.

Here, the CBT Triangle demonstrates and emphasises the link that all behaviour is preceded by a thought and feeling. It is also represented in the diagrammatic form of a triangle (see worksheet).

Why is it important? The tutor's aim is to get the client to become consciously aware, and in control, of the thoughts and feelings they have *before* any given action. The idea being that if a client can control their thoughts and feelings, then they can change their behaviour. So, for example, if the client develops more empathic thoughts and feelings for a victim, it is hoped that they will not then behave in an anti-social manner.

In this workbook, the CBT Triangle is re-named as *My Trigger Triangle*. The purpose of this is to give it a more personal feel to the offender. It is hoped that once the offender understands this exercise they can begin to 'own' their behaviour (take responsibility) as they become more consciously aware of their thoughts and feelings.

To run this exercise, we have broken it down into six easy-to-follow steps.

Step 1: Explain to the client that: "This triangle forms the basis of *all the work* that you will be doing". Here it is a good idea for the tutor to explain a little about why it is important. You can use the explanation in the tutor notes should you wish.

Step 2: Show the client the Trigger Triangle diagram.

Step 3: Explain to the client that:

- Behaviour can always be controlled and is heavily affected by our thoughts and feelings.
- If we can change any element of this triangle, then we can change all the other parts too.

Step 4: Explain that before we explore this further, we will first look to *define* what thoughts, feelings and behaviour are.

Tip: Do not look to over-complicate this definition exercise but ensure that there is clarity on (at least) a very basic level of understanding. For example, simply seek to clarify the definitions as follows:

Thoughts: The things we think about in our mind; e.g. "I am going to hit him."

Feelings: The things we feel inside; e.g. "sad, happy, angry".

Behaviour: An action, the physical part of the triangle that can be seen by others; e.g. "crying".

Tip: It is important that the client understands the difference between thoughts and feelings. For example, "I am feeling sad" is a thought about a feeling, not a feeling in itself.

Step 5: Show the client the '*My Trigger Triangle*' diagram once again and ask the client to write under the headings, using their offence as the example of behaviour, what thoughts and feelings they had before it happened.

Tip: If the offender is particularly resistant to exploring their offence in this manner, at this time, then 'roll with the resistance' and allow them to pick another example to use. However, do make sure that the offence is revisited before the completion of the 'treatment' and a trigger triangle completed for it.

Step 6: Conclude the exercise by explaining what was originally set out in the exercise. This being: *all behaviour is preceded by a thought and feeling and if we can change our thoughts and feelings then we can change our actions.*

Tip: Here you may have to check that the client understands by asking them to give a further example to summarise what has been explored.

Exercise 1 – Worksheet

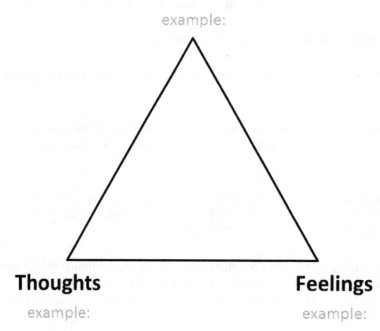

Behaviour
example:

Thoughts
example:

Feelings
example:

What is a Thought? Give an example:

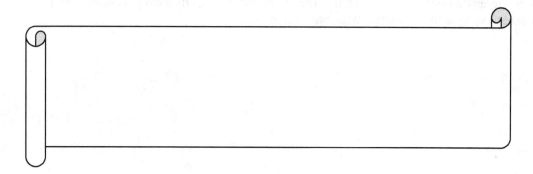

What is a Feeling? Give an example:

What is Behaviour? Give an example:

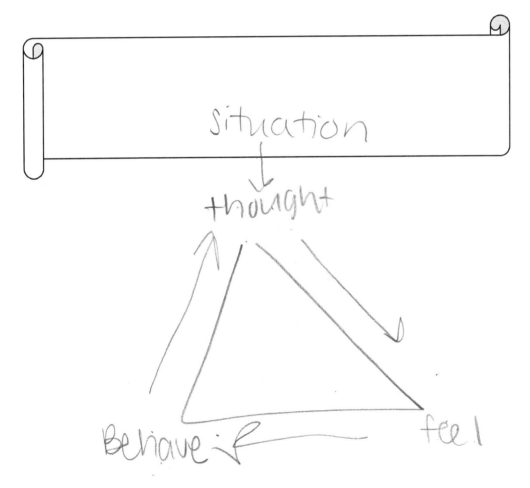

situation

thought

Behave

feel

Exercise 1a – Alternative Exercise

Step 1: Prepare nine flashcards with a picture depicting either a feeling, emotion or behaviour; three of each of these.

Step 2: Ask the offender to sort them in to three piles of 'feelings', 'thoughts' and 'behaviour'. Discuss their choices and provide guidance where appropriate.

Step 3: Ask the offender to arrange the cards on the trigger triangle at the appropriate point, depending on whether the card is depicting a thought, feeling or behaviour, so that a sequence is created relating to one particular event.

Step 4: To check understanding, ask the offender to draw three pictures on the blank cards to create their own set of 'feeling, behaviour and thought' cards based on a behaviour they do regularly. An easy one would be 'eating' – a feeling of hunger, a thought of wanting a takeaway, and a behaviour of ordering one.

Exercise 1a – Worksheet

(angry)	(happy)	(love)
I want to kick it	It's Friday!	Let's get married
Feeling	Thought	Behaviour

39

Exercise 1 – Out of Session Work

Should the tutor feel that more work on this is needed then they can present some optional work to be completed by the client outside of the session.

Step 1: Ask the client to complete a '*My Trigger Triangle*' for as many different situations as appropriate.

Step 2: Provide blank copies of the triangle and ask the offender to list - below the headings of thoughts, feelings, and behaviour - relevant examples for a specific situation that they have encountered in the week between sessions.

Tip: Generally, when this is completed, the wider the range of situations, the better the understanding of the triangle.

Exercise 1 – Out of Session - Worksheet

Give an example of when a thought and feeling made you act in a specific way

Behaviour

example:

Thoughts

example:

Feelings

example:

Exercise 1 – Review

Name at least one thing that has been learned from this exercise.

Additional Notes:

Exercise 2 – Perspective Taking

Category of exercise: Empathy Building

Tutor Notes

The next exercise looks at 'perspectives' with the client. The purpose being to stress to the client the importance of the concept that everyone can see things in a different way.

Why is perspective taking so important? Following Exercise 1, the client has now hopefully begun the journey of understanding how their thoughts and feelings impact on their behaviour. Now, with this in mind, it is equally important for the client to understand that people *do not* all have the same thoughts and feelings when any given situation arises. We are not all robots programmed to experience the same emotions and thoughts.

As an offender begins to understand that each person experiences different thoughts and feelings in any given situation they will then, arguably, be able to recognise that someone may have been affected by their offending behaviour. Even if they have previously denied, minimised, or not been able to see the impact.

In order to achieve the aims of this exercise, the tutor needs to engage the client in what can be a rather fun exercise to facilitate.

Step 1: Explain to the client that this exercise is called the *What Can You See?* and its purpose is to explore how people can see things in different ways.

Step 2: Show the client picture 1 (below) and asks them: "What do you see?" Have fun with this exercise if you can.

Tip: It is worth explaining that there is no wrong answer for what you can see here, even (and sometimes, *especially*) if you as the tutor cannot see it.

Step 3: Replicate Step 2 with the client for picture 2, and then picture 3.

Step 4: Conclude the exercise by asking the client their thoughts about the objective of that exercise and then answer the subsequent questions.

Exercise 2 – Worksheet

Picture 1

What can you see?

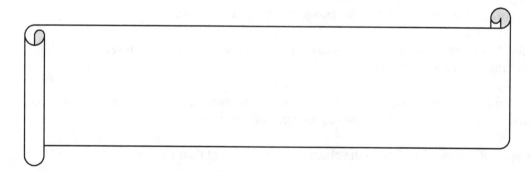

Picture 2

What can you see?

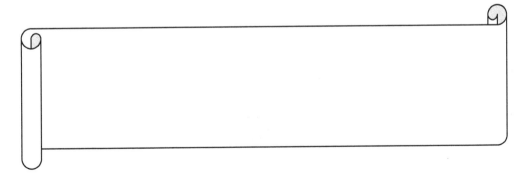

Picture 3

What can you see?

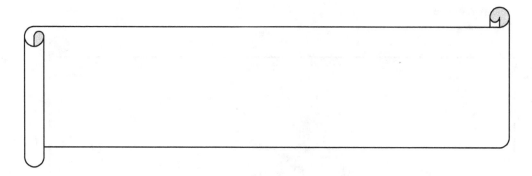

Exercise 2 – Questions

Answer the following questions:

What do you think the purpose of this exercise is?

Do you think that there is a right and wrong answer to what we see in these pictures?

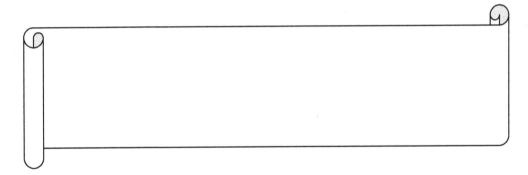

Why do I need to know how other people think and feel about my offence?

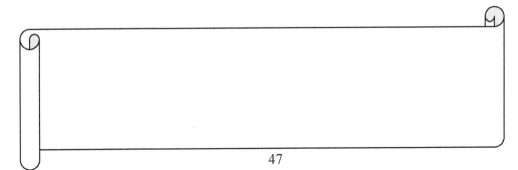

Exercise 2a – An Alternative for Different Learning Styles

If a more kinetic exercise is required (see section one) here is an alternative exercise that can be used. It is equally fun and powerful.

Step 1: Arrange the room, prior to meeting with the offender, so that there are at least three chairs with different orientations within the room.

Step 2: Make sure that something particularly eye-catching can be seen from each chair. They should be obscured or at least not as visible from the other seating positions (the simpler the better – use a colourful poster or novelty pen on a desk, for example).

Step 3: Allow the offender to sit in any of the chairs and ask them to describe what they can see when looking forwards, then rotate to the next chair, and so on.

Step 4: Ask the offender what they think the purpose of the exercise was. Explain that the description can be brief and this part of the exercise should take no more than around ten to fifteen minutes.

Tip: If the offender has difficulty, ask them to consider how and why their answers might have varied from each chair.

Exercise 2 – Out of Session Work

Should the tutor feel that more work is needed here then they can present optional work to be completed outside the session.

Step 1: Ask the offender to find an example from one of the soaps or other popular TV programmes where the script writers have used a difference in perspectives to great effect.

Step 2: Discuss with the client what they found during the next session.

Exercise 2 – Review

Name at least one thing that has been learned from this exercise.

Additional Notes:

Exercise 3 – What is a Victim?

Category of exercise: Empathy Building

Tutor Notes

By now, it is hoped that the client has begun to understand or at least appreciate the concept that everyone has a different perspective and that the victim may have been affected in some way by the offender's own behaviour.

To explore the concept of being a victim, we need to know what a victim is. Here we shall explore this subject, by first looking at what the client's own experiences of being a victim are.

We propose that one great way to build up an individual's level of victim empathy is to get them to understand that if *they* have been affected by someone else's actions so could the victim of *their* crime.

Caution: The tutor must be careful when completing this session. The tutor does not want to reinforce any idea that they (the client) are the victim of their offence. To avoid this, the tutor must place emphasis on previous experiences of perhaps "being short changed", "having a car accident which was not their fault", and so on.

To run this session effectively, the tutor will need to pre-prepare by considering possible examples the client could use. To do this, the tutor will need prior knowledge of the client's history.

Step 1: Ask the client the following: "What do you think a victim is?" When the client answers, help the client summarise what they have said. Try to get a basic definition along the lines of: "Someone who is affected by a crime or behaviour."

Tip: Ask open questions such as: "Tell me what you think a victim is?"

Step 2: Ask the client about his or her own experiences of being a victim. Follow the worksheet for this exercise as a script.

Tip: If the offender cannot think of how someone may be affected by shoplifting in point 3 of the below exercise – ask them to consider how they feel about paying extra for goods in shops so that that shop can afford security guards and recoup losses from shoplifting.

Tip: Be prepared to challenge the offender if they answer in the positive to 4a, rather than 4b.

Step 3: Discuss what the client feels was the purpose of this session and exercise. Try to conclude the session with the idea that there is no victimless crime and someone will be affected somehow by our actions.

Exercise 3 – Worksheet

Answer the following questions:

1. What is a victim?

2. In you past have you ever been a victim of an event or even a crime? Circle your answer.

Yes / No

If yes, what was it and how did it affect you? If no, continue onto the next question.

3. Do you think anyone is affected by the offence of shoplifting?

If yes, how? If no, continue to the next question.

4. Is there such thing as a crime without a victim?

    a.   If yes, why?

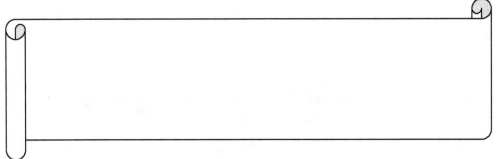

    b.   If no, why?

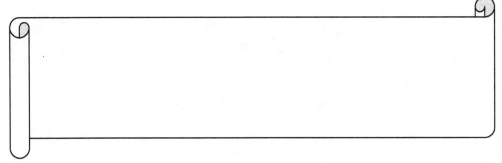

Any other comments?

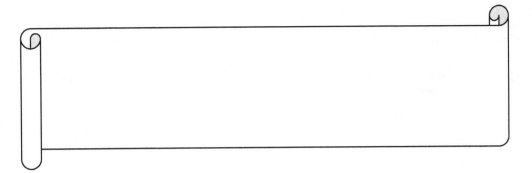

Exercise 3a – Alternative Exercise

Step 1: Arrange the room so that there are two spare chairs. Label one chair 'victim' and the other 'offender'.

Step 2: Read the excerpts on the worksheet to, or with, the offender, supporting literacy needs as appropriate.

Step 3: State one of the names from a story and ask the offender to sit in the appropriate chair as to whether that person was a victim or an offender based on the story. Repeat for all of the characters.

Step 4: Ask the offender to define a victim and add this as a sentence to the victim label on the chair. Assist as appropriate.

Exercise 3a – Worksheet

Excerpt 1

Simon had been saving for many months to buy his first motorbike. When he finally had enough money, he took great pleasure in selecting one from the local garage, in his desired colour and with metallic paint. Simon also purchased a top of the range motorcycle helmet and leathers. When he returned home, his brother Graham was jealous. During the night, Graham went into the garage, took a screwdriver from the toolbox and scraped long gouges into the side of the petrol tank. Simon was devastated in the morning when he found the damage.

Excerpt 2

Amanda was out with friends at a local night club. They were all celebrating their local football team's win that day. During the evening, Amanda became quite drunk and went to the toilets to cool down. Another group of people, including a woman called Sophie, noticed her leave her seat and also noticed that she had left her purse on the table. Sophie had recently lost her job and had no money to buy her friends a drink that evening. So Sophie went to the table and took the money out of the purse. Amanda did not notice until she went to pay for a round of drinks.

Excerpt 3

Michael was out with his friend Paul when another group of men approached them. The group of men began to taunt Michael and Paul with verbal abuse. This upset Paul greatly and he began to shout back at them. The group then responded by threatening physical violence against Paul. Michael was concerned for his friend's safety and so he decided to act first and punched one of the group, Alex. Alex suffered a broken cheekbone and had to undergo reconstructive surgery.

Excerpt 4

Liam and his friend Catherine were in town on a weekend. Neither of them had any money and both were using the trip to town to waste time as they felt they had nothing else to do. In one shop, Liam noticed that there was a sale offer for an xBox game he had wanted for a long time. Liam mentioned to Catherine that the shop was very busy and they could probably take a game without being noticed. Catherine said that she did not want to do this and risk being caught. Liam became upset at his friend and at the thought that he would not be able to get the game. He therefore decided to put the game in Catherine's bag without her noticing. On the way out of the shop, the alarms went off and Catherine was stopped by security. Liam left Catherine in the shop and ran off in to the crowds.

Exercise 3 – Out of Session Work

Should the tutor feel that more work on this topic is needed by the client then they can present optional work to be completed outside the session.

Step 1: Ask the offender to think about all the people that could be affected by the offence of driving under the influence of alcohol (drink driving).

Step 2: Ask the client to list all the people on the worksheet and to give reasons as to why each person has been affected.

Exercise 3 – Out of Session Worksheet

Who do you think could be affected by the offence of driving under the influence of alcohol (drink driving)? Add the reason for your choice next to your answer.

Who?	How? Why?

Any other comments?

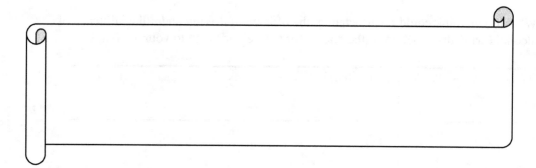

Exercise 3 – Review

Name at least one thing that has been learned from this exercise.

Additional Notes:

Exercise 4 – Direct and Indirect Victims

Category of exercise: Empathy Building

Tutor Notes

Assuming that the client has begun to build up a basic level of victim understanding in sessions 1-3, it is now appropriate to consider what are known as 'direct' and 'indirect' victims of crime.

Prior to this session, the tutor and offender may have touched upon and discussed the concept of direct and indirect victims of crime. There may have been a conversation that broached the issue of the ripple effect (see section one) and how an offender's behaviour can have a long lasting impact. This exercise helps build on this understanding or, if not previously covered, presents a good starting point to raise issues.

Step 1: Explain to the client that you are going to look at direct and indirect victims of crimes with the aim of understanding that there are no victimless crimes.

Step 2: Explain that you will be discussing the behaviour of "Smashing up a telephone box".

Step 3: Ask the client to complete the below questionnaire with you whilst considering the behaviour from Step 2.

When undertaking Step 3, you should place an emphasis on this being an example of an offence with an *indirect* victim e.g. someone whom the offender would not commonly think of as being affected (due to the nature of the offence).

Step 4: Then, ask the client to think of an offence with a *direct victim*. You should let the client decide on the example, but provide assistance if the client is struggling.

Exercise 4 – Worksheet

Answer the following questions:

Who is affected by the smashing of a telephone box?

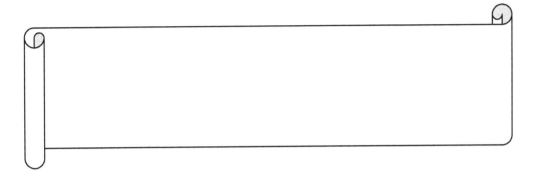

How are they affected?

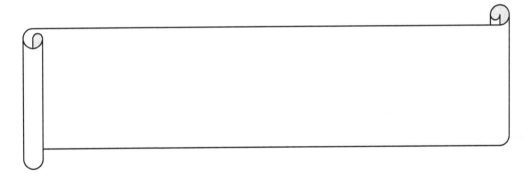

Who pays?

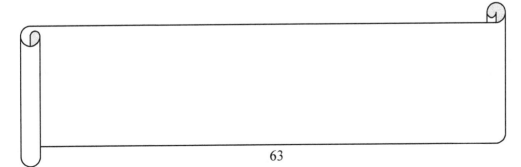

Any other comments?

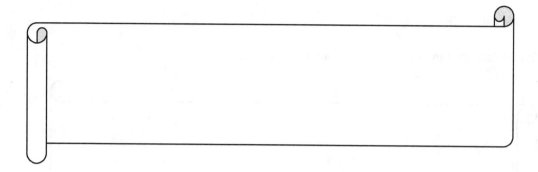

Now, think of an offence with a *direct victim*.

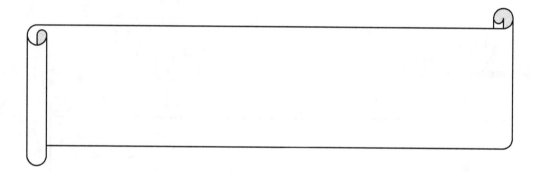

Answer the following questions:

Who is affected by this offence?

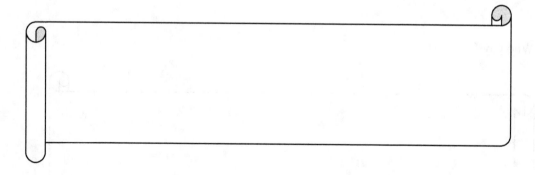

How are they affected?

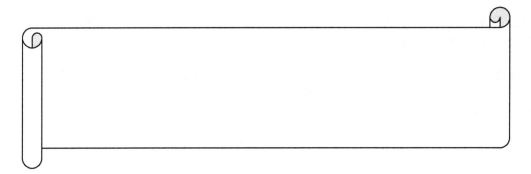

Who pays?

Any other comments?

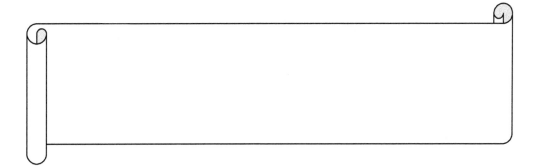

Exercise 4a – Alternative Exercise

Step 1: Write down an offence without an obvious direct victim, such as graffiti, on the centre of a flipchart sheet in a black pen.

Step 2: With the offender discuss people that may be affected by, or who may notice, this offence. Using a 'brainstorming' style of presentation, write *who* may be affected in one colour and *how* they may be affected in another.

Tip: There is likely to be more than one example of 'who' for the crime.

Step 3: Ask the offender to repeat the exercise for both an offence with no obvious direct victim and for an offence with a direct victim, allowing them to write the 'who' and 'how'. Assist with literacy needs as appropriate.

Step 4: Using the diagrams, discuss the points raised with the offender to ensure their understanding of the concepts of direct and indirect victims.

Exercise 4a – Worksheet Example

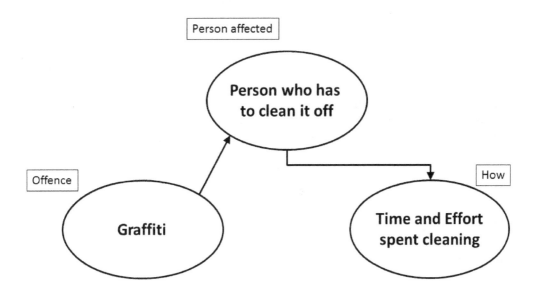

Exercise 4 – Out of Session Work

Should the tutor feel that more work on this topic is needed by the client then they can present optional work to be completed outside the session.

Step 1: Consider (with the help of the client) a current and relevant example of an offence with indirect victims. Try to use an example from which the media is widely reporting (for example, the MPs' expenses scandal where MPs fraudulently claimed money back from the taxpayer, or the 'horsemeat scandal' where horsemeat was labelled as beef).

Step 2: Thinking more about the chosen example, ask the offender to consider and answer the following questions which should be answered on the out of session worksheet. The worksheet can either be given to the offender or completed with the tutor at the next session.

- Do they consider themselves to be a victim of these offences?
- Why?
- How were they affected?
- Does the fact that they would be considered an indirect victim of these offences lessen their annoyance/anger or the impact of the offence?

Exercise 4 – Out of Session Worksheet

Which offence, incident or event are you considering?

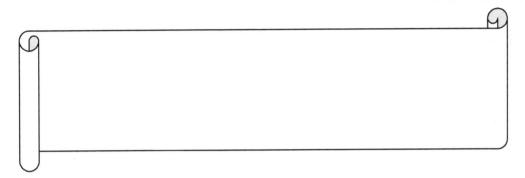

Do you consider yourself to be a victim of these offences?   Yes / No

Why?

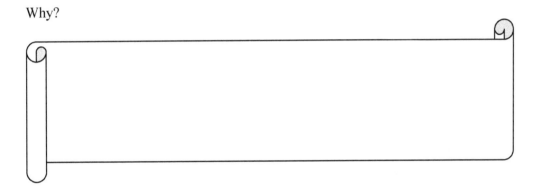

How were you affected?

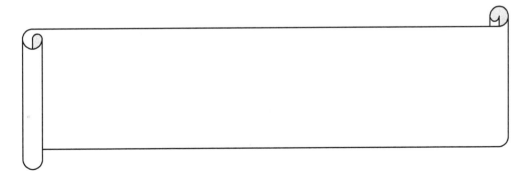

Does the fact that you would be considered an indirect victim of these offences lessen your annoyance/anger or the impact of the offence?

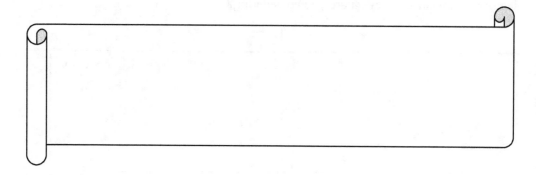

Exercise 4 – Review

Name at least one thing that has been learned from this exercise.

Additional Notes:

Exercise 5 – Effects of Crime on Different People

Category of exercise: Empathy Building

Tutor notes

In this session, a more in-depth understanding of how crime affects different people in different ways will be explored. This session combines most of the work done so far on perspective taking so the facilitator is encouraged to reflect back with the client on key aspects through discussion.

Step 1: Explain that: "We are now going to look at *how* crime affects different people in different ways."

Step 2: Show the client the table on the worksheet (below) and ask the client to complete it. Here the tutor should explain that: "In this table, you (the client) will see a number of different people who *could* be affected by a particular offence. If you agree, how do you think they were affected?"

Step 3: The client completes the table.

Step 4: Explore the answers the client has given, with the client.

Tip: The tutor should look for answers which incorporate all aspects of the previously explored *trigger triangle*. So, for example, you should ask questions along the lines of: "How did the young person feel, think and behave?"

Step 5: Explore direct and indirect victims. Ask whether the client feels any of those identified in the table are direct or indirect victims, and why.

Tip: There is some room for discussion about whether a person's closeness to the offence and victims, in both relationships and physical distance, affects the impact of the offence. Also, be wary of stereotypical answers and be prepared to challenge them. Pensioners are not only/just scared of youths, despite what the media may portray. And vandalism is not just committed by youths.

Exercise 5 – Worksheet

Offences	Young Person	Single Mother	Pensioner	Police Officer	Family
Vandalism of Car					
Burglary					
Possession of Drugs					
Shoplifting					
Drink Driving					
Rape					

Exercise 5a – Alternative Exercise

This exercise is a little more prescriptive in terms of the potential impact that crime may have on a victim. The idea behind this alternative is to reduce the 'open-endedness' of the question. Whilst open questions are usually the best strategy in enabling offenders, in some cases it may be that too much choice (or potential for answer) is actually paralysing. It may therefore be useful to complete the main exercise following this one, if the practitioner feels that there has been a sufficient increase in understanding.

Step 1: Prior to the session, cut out the cards from the worksheet

Step 2: With the offender, pick an 'offence type' and place this on the table.

Step 3: Place the 'victim cards' in a row underneath this heading. Ask the offender to place any 'effect' cards underneath the victim card to which they feel the effect is applicable.

Step 4: If the offender feels that an effect may apply to more than one victim, or even apply to none, then this should be explored by the practitioner through discussion.

Step 5: Go through the offender's choices and ask them why they have paired the cards as they have.

Tip: Use the trigger triangle to explore the 'victims' thoughts, feelings and behaviour if the offender is struggling to explain their choice.

Exercise 5a – Worksheet

Shoplifting	Common Assault	Drink Driving	Rape	Manslaughter
Pensioner	Single female	Parent	Young child	Male youth
Too afraid to go out alone	Only goes shopping in the day	Doesn't celebrate Christmas anymore	Lost job	Stereotyped by others in the community
Not able to support family anymore	Can't afford to buy from a particular shop	Depression	Loss of marriage /partnership	Serious injury
Loss of income	Feelings of isolation	Loss of friendships	Attending Court	Difficulties explaining need for support to others

Exercise 5 – Out of Session Work

Should the tutor feel that more work on this topic is needed by the client then they can present optional work to be completed outside the session.

Step 1: Provide the client with a copy of the table (below) which is empty of offence types, but which leaves the people categories in.

Step 2: Discuss with the offender, prior to the end of the session, what offences could go into the table when they are completing it. It is important here for the tutor to try to steer the suggestions to areas outside offending behaviour committed by the offender.

Step 3: Review the completed table during the next session.

Exercise 5 – Out of Session Worksheet

Offences	Young Person	Single Mother	Pensioner	Police Officer	Family

Exercise 5 – Review

Name at least one thing that has been learned from this exercise.

Additional Notes:

Exercise 6 – My Offence

Category of exercise: Self Awareness

Tutor Notes

Up until now, should the tutor have followed the exercises sequentially, it will be clear that much of the emphasis has been on looking at how *others* (people who the offender does not know) have been affected by crime.

Now, the tutor will be seeking to help the offender understand how their (the offender's) behaviour can have a negative impact on those close to them, as well as the offender as an individual. The purpose of this process is to help build up the client's *consequential thinking*.

In order to undertake this exercise, it is important to focus on using an example of the offender's own criminal behaviour that they want, or are at least willing, to discuss. This exercise methodology is taken from Hussey (2012) and utilises the concept of brainstorming.

Step 1: Explain that the client will now be completing an exercise focused on an offence that they have committed - that they want to discuss.

Step 2: Explain that this exercise is called "brainstorming". The idea being to simply generate lots of alternatives for an idea. The tutor should also explain that no answer is wrong but challenge any inappropriate comments.

Tip: Try to *sell* this exercise as being about learning to generate lots of different ideas from one statement or question. Explain how it is really effective in problem solving.

Step 3: Use the worksheet for this exercise. The tutor should ask the client to think about their offence or a recent offence, and consider how it has affected them, their family, the victim(s), and the victim's family. When the client answers, the tutor should draw a line from the statement in the circle with the answer at the end. For example:

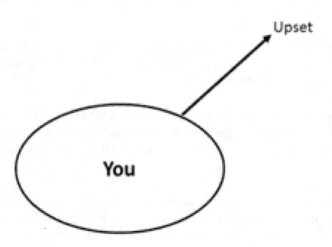

Exercise 6 – Worksheet

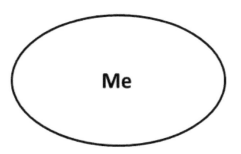

Exercise 6 – Worksheet

My Victim

My Victim's
Family

Exercise 6a – Alternative Exercise

This exercise is based mainly on discussion and it is anticipated that the practitioner will be taking the notes.

Note: Prior to the session, it is important that the practitioner has read through the statements and only uses statements which are appropriate to the offender's situation and the purpose of the exercise. The idea of this exercise is not to try to draw out anti-social answers from the offender!

Step 1: Cut out each of the statements so that they are individual slips. Read the statement to the offender and ask them to comment whether it is 'true' or 'false'. Place the cards into two piles of 'true' and 'false' statements.

Step 2: Take one of the piles and revisit each of the statements. Ask the offender to explain why they felt it was true/false. Challenge inappropriate answers and allow the offender to change their mind, *if they choose to.*

Step 3: If any anti-social or inappropriate answers remain, use the trigger triangle to explore with the offender why you, as the practitioner, have a difference of perspective.

Tip: Use Motivational Interviewing at this stage and do not attempt to force the offender to change their mind. Remember 'roll with resistance' (see section one).

True or false

Exercise 6a – Worksheet

There was no impact on the victim from my offence
My parents did not mind my offending behaviour
Having a criminal record will not affect my future
The victim did not suffer any long term effects
The victim's family were concerned for the victim's welfare
The court case cost me/my parents time and money
Court was a daunting experience for my parents
Court was a daunting experience for me
Court was a daunting experience for my victim's family
My behaviour set a good example for my siblings/children
There was no emotional distress associated with my offending
There was no financial distress associated with my offending
There were no injuries caused through my actions

Only the victim suffered any inconvenience
My family have not suffered any long term effects from my behaviour
My housing status will not be affected
The type of offence I committed is expected of me by 'society'
The prospect of going to/returning to prison concerns me
My victim's family may have concerns about meeting me in the future

Exercise 6 – Out of Session Work

Should the tutor feel that more work on this topic is needed by the client then they can present optional work to be completed outside the session.

Step 1: Ask the client to think about their most recent offence.

Step 2: Ask the client who was involved in the offence from arrest onwards. For example: Police, Solicitors, Judges, Prison, etc.

Step 3: Ask the client to complete the following worksheet to think about how much money their offence may have 'cost' the community.

Step 4: The client should try to add up the total cost. Of course with this exercise, there is no correct answer with regards to cost – this would simply be too difficult to figure out. The tutor should simply try to gain an estimate to emphasise the point. If the offender is able to recognise that a Police Officer was involved in their offence for a day, then the 'cost' is paying that Officer's wage for the day, etc.

Exercise 6 – Out of Session Worksheet

Who? (explain who and what the cost is for)	How much?
me	
family	
officer	
post office	
court people	
Total Cost:	

Exercise 6 – Review

Name at least one thing that has been learned from this exercise.

Additional Notes:

Exercise 7 – The Ripple Effect

Category of exercise: Self Awareness

Tutor Notes

In this exercise the tutor will explore what is known as the ripple effect. Namely, *when an offender commits a crime, its impact cascades across to other people or even the whole community.*

The idea of this exercise is to try to get the offender to see and understand that any offence impacts not only on the client but other people as well.

Step 1: Show the client the ripple diagram.

Step 2: Explain to the client how the diagram works. This being: *The victim occupies the inner circle, their family the next layer, and so on, until the very outer layer is more remote such as 'government policies'.*

Note: The idea is explained as being like the impact of dropping a stone in a pond; the strongest impact is where the stone falls, but the river bank still feels the ripple and enough ripples will eventually lead to erosion.

Step 3: Ask the client to think of as many effects, as far reaching as possible, for all the elements of the circles.

Tip: To engage a more resistant offender, present this exercise as a challenge to get them to think of just how far they can imagine the impact of their behaviour reaching. This approach may not be suitable in all cases and the practitioner will need to use their professional judgment. Always enable the offender to understand the negativity attached to such wide reaching consequences - the main message being that it is up to them as to whether their 'importance' to others or within society is of a negative or positive influence.

Exercise 7 – Example Diagram

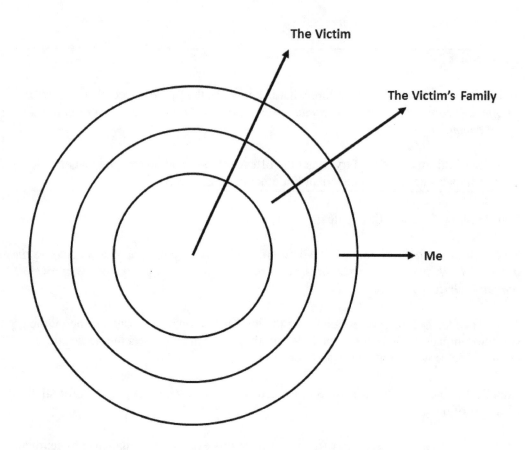

Exercise 7 – Worksheet

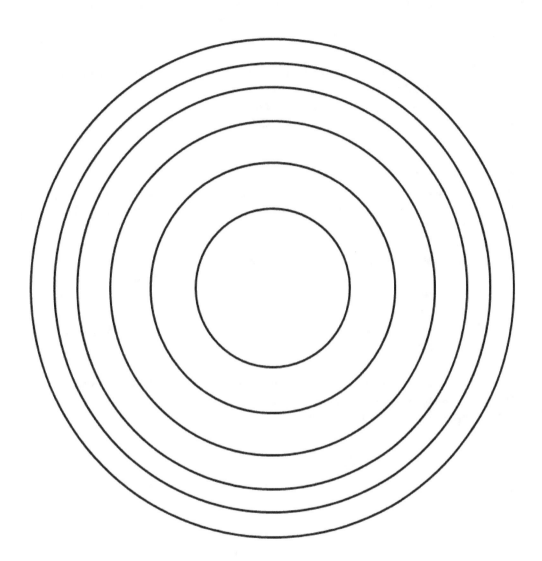

Exercise 7a – Alternative Exercise

Step 1: The tutor should clear the room of obstacles so there is a fair sized floor space available. When this is done, the tutor should lay out sections of rope or string in concentric circles (like in worksheet 7). Try to have *at least* four circles.

Step 2: The tutor should have several cards ready, or prepare them with the offender. On each card, the facilitator or client should write the names of different people who could be affected by their offence or behaviour. The facilitator here should also encourage the client to consider organisations or communities that have been affected. Again, write these on the cards.

Step 3: Ask the offender to place the cards in the circles on the floor. Here the tutor explains that the centre circle should represent the 'centre' of the crime and so people placed here feel the greatest impact from it. The further away from the centre, the more reduced the impact felt.

Note: The idea needs to be explained as being like the impact of dropping a stone in a pond; the strongest impact is where the stone falls, but the bank still feels the ripple and enough ripples will eventually lead to erosion.

Step 4: The facilitator should then discuss with the offender the reasons why they made the choices they did.

Note: There will always be room for debate towards the edges of the circles but challenge any answers which appear anti-social or wide of the mark such as placing the victim anywhere but the centre.

Exercise 7 – Out Of Session Work

Should the tutor feel that more work on this topic is needed by the client then they can present optional work to be completed outside the session.

Step 1: Provide the offender with a blank ripple diagram.

Step 2: Ask them to consider a person of whom they think highly; anyone from a celebrity to a family member is appropriate.

Step 3: Get the offender to complete the ripple diagram to show both who, and how, the chosen person has an impact on those around them.

Step 4: Review the diagram at the next session.

Exercise 7 – Review

Name at least one thing that has been learned from this exercise.

Additional Notes:

Exercise 8 – Broken Windows

Category of exercise: Self Awareness and Empathy

(Adapted from the 'Broken Window Theory' by Wilson and Kelling 1982, cited in Giddens, A. (2001) Sociology (4th Ed.) Oxford: Polity Press/Blackwell Publishers)

Tutor notes

Broken Windows is a mainly discussion-based exercise which aims to give the offender an understanding of broken window theory and, as such, the longitudinal impact of offending on an area.

It is useful to have completed Exercise 7 prior to this one, as the offender should be able to think of extended consequences for their behaviour, beyond direct victims.

Step 1: Ask the offender to imagine a newly empty factory. Continue to describe a scenario where a passer-by notices a broken window in the factory. Ask the offender what that person's options are regarding the window. Try to elicit responses such as "report it to the council" or "ignore it" or "nothing".

Step 2: Write one of the *negative* behavioural responses (such as "ignore") on one of the windows of the factory on the worksheet. This now counts as another 'broken window' on the factory.

Step 3: Give examples of other people or groups who may go past or see the factory and ask the offender to consider what responses or thoughts these people may have. Write a summary of each *negative* point across other windows. Keep the points expanding to more and more indirect and generalised consequences.

Tip: The points need to be sequential so that, at the end, the offender is able to see a 'knock on' cumulative effect deriving from something as simple as a broken window.

Examples may be:

- A group of youths and the response may be to try and break another window. The tutor would then write 'anti-social behaviour' across another window.
- A young executive couple deciding not to buy a house in the area as it looks 'a bit rough'. The tutor can then write 'negative assumptions' on another window.
- Current residents lose interest in maintaining properties or gardens in a 'rough' area. Write 'rough area' on another window.
- The head of the neighbourhood watch assuming that there has been an increase in anti-social behaviour recently, asks Police to increase patrols in the area. Write 'bad reputation' on another window.

95

- Community events are cancelled through fear of 'trouble'. Write 'malicious rumours' on another window.
- Business entrepreneurs decide not to invest locally for fear of the degeneration of the area and the factory stays empty. Write 'loss of investment' on another window.

Each time the tutor writes on a window, that window is then considered as 'broken'.

Step 4: refocus the discussion on what the initial problem was – a simple broken window – and how this led to assumptions, negativity, and a feeling of a loss of care.

The main message here is that no one broken window (or one negative action/behaviour) in itself was particularly problematic but the cumulative effect was such that the whole was greater than the sum of its parts. Also, none of the negative statements were necessarily true at the time they were made but each became a self-fulfilling prophecy once there.

Then turn this on its head – if negative thoughts and behaviour can cause these effects, no matter how exaggerated it is in the exercise, then what could positive behaviour and thoughts do for an area and for the people in the area…

Exercise 8 – Worksheet

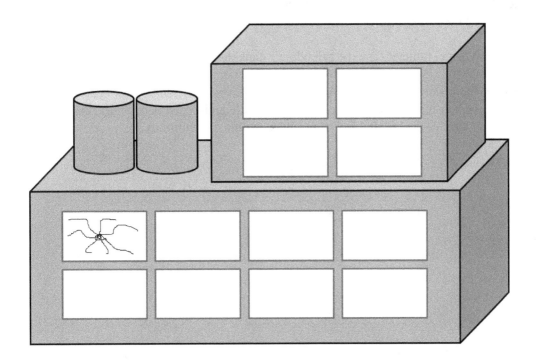

Exercise 8a – Alternative Exercise

From snowflake to avalanche.

Step 1: Prior to the session, the practitioner needs to make several cubes (the net of a cube is provided on the worksheet).

Step 2: Ask the offender to write as many impacts of anti-social behaviour as they can think of on each of the cubes (one on each cube, not per side).

Step 3: When completed, ask the offender to stack the cubes up as a tower.

Step 4: The tower will eventually topple. Discuss with the offender how even small actions, such as placing one cube on another or little anti-social behaviours, can lead to a big event, such as the 'avalanche' or problems within a community.

Exercise 8a – Worksheet

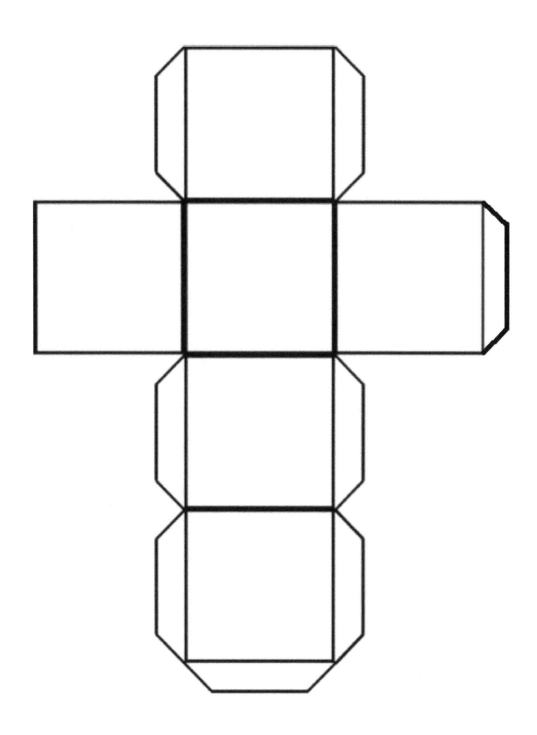

Exercise 8 – Out of Session Work

In order to build on the understanding that big events are usually made of small constituent parts, the following out of session work may be useful.

Step 1: Ask the offender to think of a big news story in the media at the moment and write it in the centre of the worksheet.

Step 2: Ask the offender to complete the rest of the worksheet out of session. Going *outwards* on the worksheet, reducing the 'big' event into smaller contributory factors, as in a brainstorming style.

Exercise 8 – Out of Session Worksheet

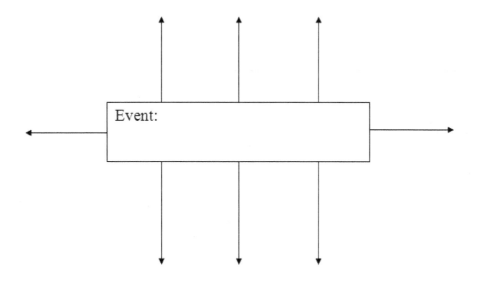

Exercise 8 – Review

Name at least one thing that has been learned from this exercise.

Additional Notes:

Exercise 9 – The Offender as the Victim

Category of exercise: Self Awareness

Tutor notes

An important part of increasing victim empathy is the ability of the offender to understand the existence of different perspectives and using this knowledge when assessing situations and deciding on a course of action. This exercise requires the offender to role-play being a victim - the idea being that if they are able to take a step in the victim's shoes, they will start to be able to do this when faced with a potential offending situation in the future. If the working relationship and willingness is there, and the practitioner feels it is appropriate, the offender can play their own victim.

Note: Be careful that the offender is actually willing and does not end up minimising the impact on the victim, justifying their offence through victim blaming, or indeed gaining pleasure through reliving the offence.

Step 1: Using the questions from the worksheet, ask the offender to talk through the offence from the perspective of the victim.

Step 2: Assist the offender in structuring the account of the 'victim' so that it covers the impact of the offence from immediate, short term, medium term and projected long term positions.

Tip: Not all of the suggested questions will be appropriate. The practitioner needs to pick and choose as fits with the offence type and the offender. The overall idea is to create a timeline of the *impact* of the offence, not just the physical behaviours.

Step 3: Create a timeline diagram once the discussion is completed. The practitioner will need to take notes during the discussion.

Tip: The 'My *Trigger Triangle*' can be used to assist the offender in extrapolating how a change in thoughts or feelings of the victim may lead to a change in behaviours.

Step 4: Discuss with the offender how they feel about each of the points raised and how they would like to answer these as themselves, should they ever meet with the victim.

Timeline example for an offence of robbery:

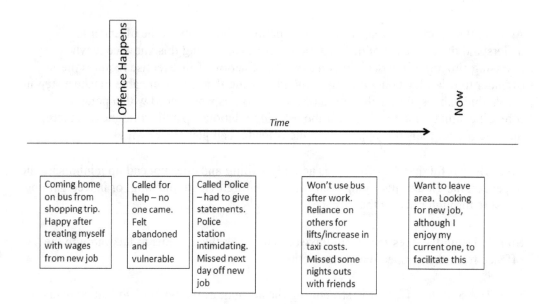

Offence Happens

Now

Time

| Coming home on bus from shopping trip. Happy after treating myself with wages from new job | Called for help – no one came. Felt abandoned and vulnerable | Called Police – had to give statements. Police station intimidating. Missed next day off new job | Won't use bus after work. Reliance on others for lifts/increase in taxi costs. Missed some nights outs with friends | Want to leave area. Looking for new job, although I enjoy my current one, to facilitate this |

Exercise 9 – Worksheet

Questions to pose to the offender in role as a/the victim:

What were you doing prior to the offence?

How did the offender come to your notice, or you to theirs?

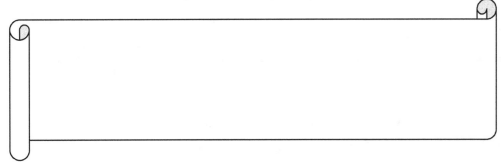

Describe the offence.

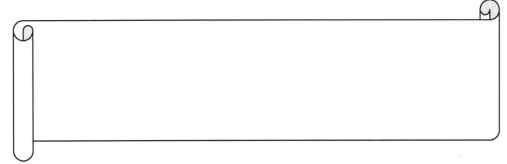

How did this make you feel?

What was your immediate response/behaviour?

How did you feel the next day?

Have you changed any of your plans, or usual activities, to avoid a recurrence of the offence?

Where do you think you will be in one year from now? And five years? Will you continue to abide by the changes you have made?

How have your friends and/or family responded?

Exercise 9a – Alternative Exercise

Step 1: Show the offender the three outlines of a person on the worksheets. Ask the offender to label the outline person as their victim, if they do not know the name then ask them to give the victim a name. Also ask the offender to personalise the outlines for the victim; give them clothes, a face, hair, and so on.

Caution: DO NOT allow the offender to deface the outline or graffiti it. Devil horns or a comedic moustache are not appropriate. It may be that the practitioner needs to discuss re-victimisation with the offender if this behaviour occurs.

Step 2: Label one outline 'immediate effects', another 'medium term effects' and the third 'long term effects'.

Step 3: Ask the offender to write around the edge of the outline the impact that *their* offence had on *their* victim. Assist with literacy needs as appropriate.

Tip: Keep the offender specific to the circumstances of their offence. This is not an exercise on the general impact of offending on victims.

Step 4: Ask the offender to read the effects they have written to you, as the practitioner, in role as the victim (so using 'I statements': I felt scared and so on) in order from short term effect through to long term effects.

Exercise 9a – Worksheet

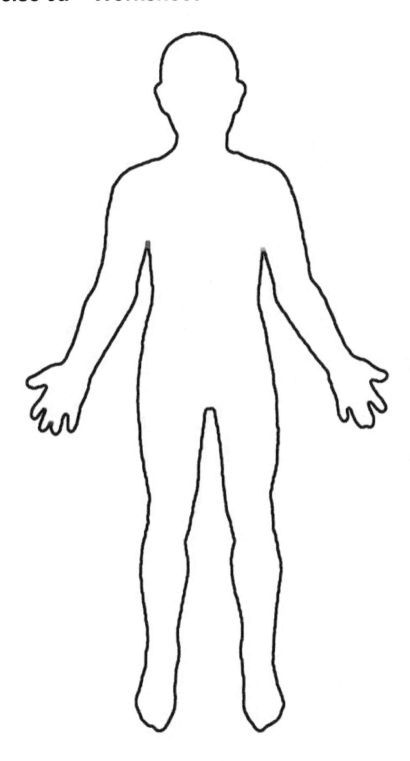

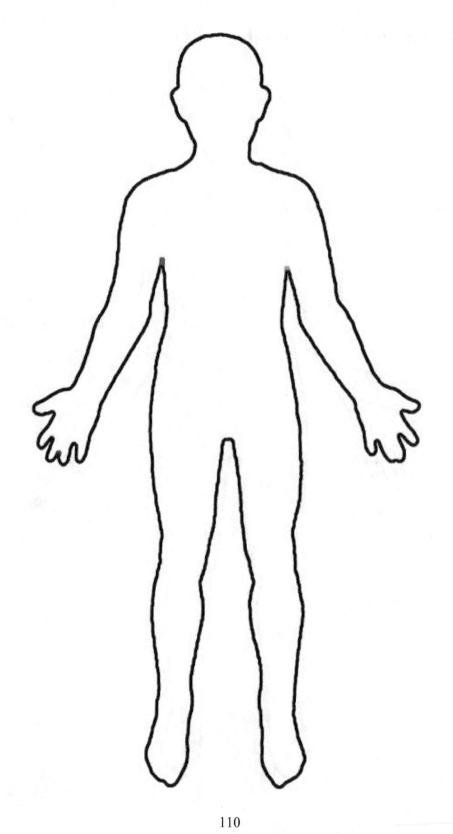

110

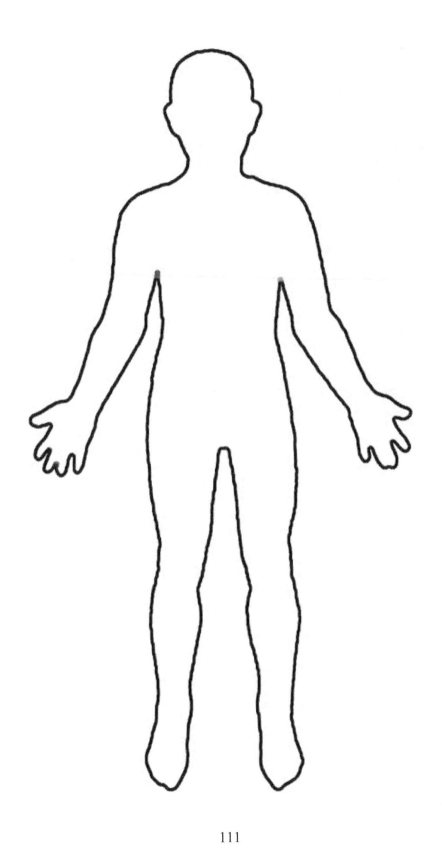

Exercise 9 – Out of Session Work

Step 1: Remind the offender of the main skill used in the exercise in the session, namely perspective taking.

Step 2: Ask the offender to pick any interesting scenarios or situations they encounter during their week (these do not have to be based on offending/anti-social behaviour) and note the following:

- How many different perspectives there may have been
- How their perspective differed from the others
- Why they think there may have been a difference of opinions
- How it was resolved

Exercise 9 – Out of Session Worksheet

Scenario:

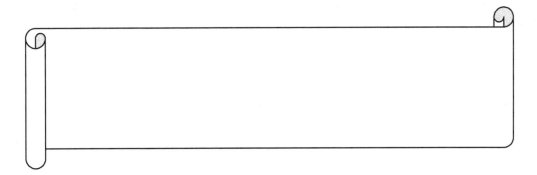

How many different perspectives were there? Briefly describe them.

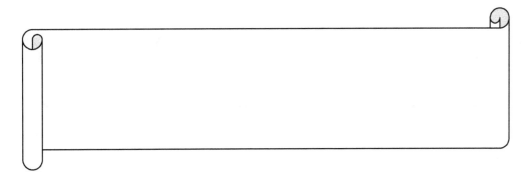

How did your perspective differ from the others?

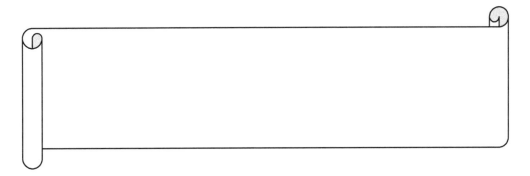

Why do you think there were differences of opinions?

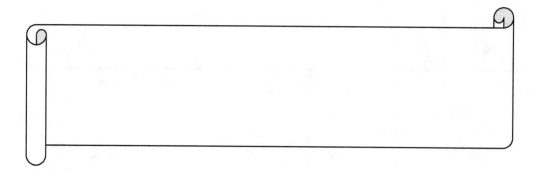

How it was resolved? Was this a satisfactory outcome for all the people involved?

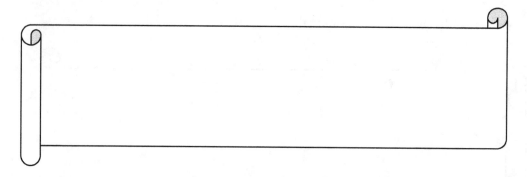

Exercise 9 – Review

Name at least one thing that has been learned from this exercise.

Additional Notes:

Exercise 10 – The Letter

Category of exercise: Self Awareness and Empathy Building

Tutor Notes

The idea behind *The Letter* is that it works through the key points that a victim is likely to want acknowledged and answered; therefore the offender must use their, hopefully increased, ability to take the victim's perspective and demonstrate empathy towards them.

Where there are literacy difficulties, the practitioner should act as scribe. In most cases, it would be beneficial for the practitioner to type up the *completed* letter, ready for the next session. Whilst it is unlikely to be sent, this demonstrates to the offender that their apology is valuable, and also allows them to keep a copy.

It is also likely to be very helpful for the offender to go through a structure of how to set this letter out. A blank piece of paper can be very intimidating. A suggested structure is given below but this is not the only or 'correct' way to do it. It can and should be adapted for each individual offender.

Tip: Whilst it may be tempting to guide and instruct the offender in the writing, and indeed some may look for a high level of support in the wording, the point of this exercise is for the offender to put their voice down on paper. Vocabulary, grammar and so on can be revised at a later time. At the first run through, allow the offender free rein. This will also assist in an assessment of the levels of responsibility taking.

Crucial points for the practitioner are:

- This is not an exercise to allow the offender to point out how the victim was to blame or influential in the commissioning of the offence.

- This is not an opportunity for the offender to paint a 'poor me' picture, or demonstrate a low level of responsibility for their choices/actions.

- It should not be a missive of the offender's life culminating in the point of the offence.

- There is no need to describe the offence, the victim was there…

Step 1: Read the suggested questions to the offender and ask them to write or dictate their thoughts for each point.

Step 2: Ask the offender to create a letter from their answers to the questions.

Step 3: Once completed, the practitioner should read it back to the offender and then ask them for their feedback. Ask them to consider how the victim may receive it. Does their letter sound sincere? If not, why not?

Note: If the offender feels they have committed an offence with no *direct* victims, through discussion with them, chose an indirect victim to address the letter to. Or address the letter to a potential/future employer

Tip: Avoid reification of institutions; it is generally not appropriate to address a letter to 'society at large'.

Exercise 10 – Worksheet

Dear _____

(consider which term of address is most appropriate, for example Mr Jones or Bob)

Why is the letter being written?

What has motivated the writing of the letter?

Why do you want to/feel the need to contact the victim?

Are there any reassurances that you can give to the victim?

Have you made any changes to your life since the commissioning of the offence?

Is there anything else that you feel the victim would *benefit* from knowing?

How are you going to sign off the letter? Consider what is most appropriate - *Yours Sincerely, Yours Faithfully*, and so on. *Best Wishes* and other colloquial endings are unlikely to be appropriate.

Exercise 10a – Alternative Exercise

The importance of this exercise is for the offender to be able to get their thoughts relating to victim empathy into a structured form which can be revisited and which is specific to their victim; hence the letter form. If, as a practitioner, you feel that the offender requires a different approach to this exercise, then adapting the presentation of the session is appropriate. However, the end game needs to be a letter addressed specifically to a victim and containing apologies and empathy from the offender for the experience.

Different approaches to the presentation of this exercise may include using flipcharts to brainstorm answers onto the worksheet, or taking a laptop to the session so that either the offender or the practitioner can write the letter, using the worksheet as simply a prompt.

Finally, an offender may wish to just write their own letter with no support from the practitioner. If this is case then roll with it (see section one 'motivational interviewing'). Read through the letter once completed and challenge any inappropriate comments or points. Issues to look out for will include:

- Minimising the offence or telling the victim how they should have reacted at the time/since.
- Justifying their behaviour through a lengthy explanation of the reasons behind the offence.
- Any elements of blame towards others who were present or the victim themselves.
- Any statements which indicate a lack of taking responsibility. Look out for sentences which contain 'just' or 'only'.

Exercise 10 – Out of Session Work

Note: It is very important that this is completed only with a person that the offender feels they can trust to listen and be non-judgemental. Therefore the practitioner must use their professional judgement as to whether this is a suitable exercise to set.

Step 1: Ask the offender to read their letter, completed within the session, to someone they can trust.

Step 2: Ask the offender to provide feedback to the practitioner in the next session as to how the letter was received and any feedback given by the third person.

Tip: Prior to completing Step 2, the practitioner needs to consider how they will address any potential situations where the third person's feedback is inappropriate. For example, if the feedback reinforces some of the anti-social notions the offender previously demonstrated.

Exercise 10 – Review

Name at least one thing that has been learned from this exercise.

Additional Notes:

Exercise 11 – The 'What If' Flowchart

Category of exercise: Self Awareness

Tutor Notes

The idea of this exercise is to combine all the ideas of victim awareness in a more generalised way with the consequences of our actions. This should help give the offender an idea of 'the point' of increasing victim awareness.

Depending on the depth of discussion between the offender and the practitioner, and the abilities of the offender, this exercise may be best explored over several sessions. This would also provide for out of session work to be set.

Step 1: The facilitator asks the client to think of a situation that they feel encourages their offending or problematic behaviour. This is known as a *high risk* situation. An example of a high risk situation could be: "Drinking alcohol with friends in a park."

Note: The high risk situation will now be the starting block for completing a flow chart. The facilitator should write the high risk situation in a circle at the top of a piece of A4 paper and put a circle around it.

Step 2: The facilitator should now explore with the client as many possible options as they can with regards to what *could* happen. Using the example of "Drinking alcohol with friends in a park", some possible options could be getting drunk, or not simply not getting drunk.

Step 3: The facilitator should ask the client to consider again what the consequences would be for each resulting behaviour identified in step 2. Using our getting drunk example, some of the possible resulting behaviours could be *going home* or perhaps *going into town*.

Step 4: The facilitator again asks the offender to consider further possible consequences of what could happen for each circumstance they give in step 3. Repeat this process until a final resulting offending/antisocial behaviour is reached as one of the consequences.

Step 5: Explore with the client all the possible consequences the final resulting negative behaviour has to the following people: themselves, friends, the possible victim, the victim's family and the community. These consequences can be immediate, short term, medium term and long term

An example flow chart is given to illustrate the process. This can be shared with the offender if the tutor feels it will be of benefit. Especially if they are a visual learner.

Exercise 11 – Example Worksheet

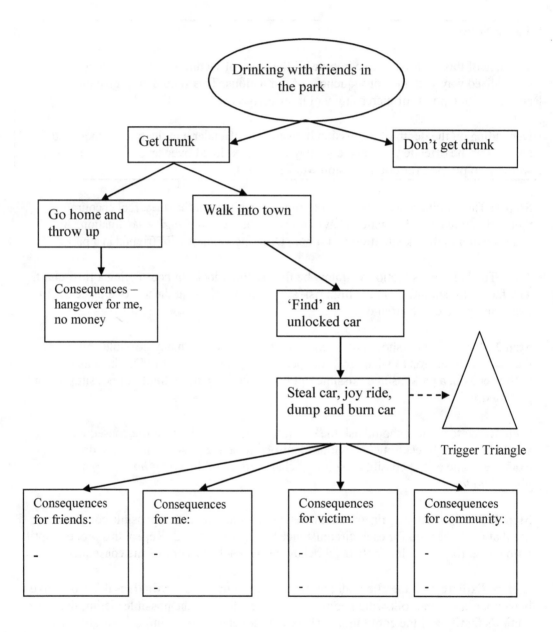

Exercise 11 – Worksheet

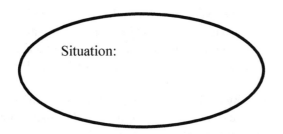

Situation:

Exercise 11a – Alternative Exercise

As with exercise 5, this alternative exercise reduces the 'open-endedness' of the exercise for those clients who might otherwise find it too challenging. However, once there is an understanding developed through completing this exercise, the practitioner may choose to then complete exercise 11; using this alternative very much as a 'lead in'.

This exercise is designed as a physical 'walkthrough' of decision making and consequences. The offender should be actually walking on the sheets of paper as they go through the exercise. There is some preparation required by the tutor prior to the session.

Step 1: Prior to the session, the tutor needs to write out the 'steps'(or choices) of a problematic behaviour *relevant* to the offender on sheets of A4 paper. One step per piece of paper. An example is given in the worksheet below. Start with a potentially risky situation such as 'bored at home – call friends and go into town.' The next two sheets will have either a 'yes' or 'no' on one side so that the offender can step forwards to the direction of their answer – the reverse of the sheet will need the consequences of that yes or no answer. Such as, on the 'yes' sheet – 'meet friends in town' or on the 'no' sheet – 'stay home and choose another activity'.

Tip: The idea of this exercise is that the offender takes a step forwards down the stepping stones per decision made – so each piece of paper needs to provide either a question or an answer.

Step 2: Whether a decision allows the offender to 'step away' from the risky situation or whether they complete the path and end up at an offending behaviour - they then need to complete a flipchart sheet for the consequences of that decision. Prepare a flipchart sheet with a title heading 'consequences' and then subheadings of 'short term', 'medium term' and 'long term' consequences, and rows down the left hand side of 'me', 'my friends', 'my family', 'my victim' and 'my victim's family' (creating a chart for the client to complete).

Note: Where the offender has chosen a path that leads them away from offending, the answer to the consequences for 'victim' are 'no negative ones'!

Step 3: In preparation for the session, lay out the paper face down so that it creates a 'path' with 'crossroads' where decisions need to be made (see worksheet for an illustration of this). Where a sheet has a 'yes' or 'no' on one side, this is the side that faces up. The start of the path is the initial, potentially risky, situation.

Step 4: Starting at the first page, ask the offender to turn it over and answer the question. They then need to step forwards in the direction decided by their answer. Then turn over the sheet of paper they have moved to and answer that question, again moving forwards in the direction dictated by their answer.

Step 5: Repeat the above until the offender reaches the end of one of the paths. Using the sheet of flipchart paper, ask them to write the consequences of their final behaviour for each of the categories in the rows.

Tip: The offender can 're-run' the path to come to different conclusions as many times as the practitioner feels appropriate simply by turning the sheets back over. Always complete a new flipchart sheet for the consequences for each re-run though.

Exercise 11a – Worksheet

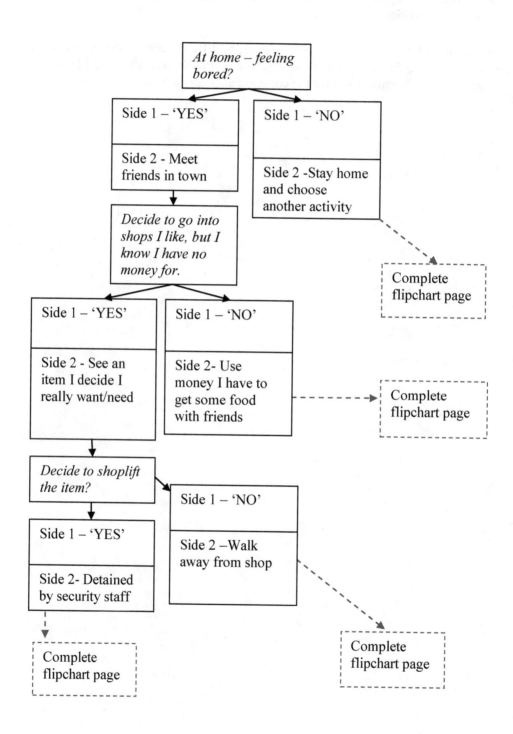

Exercise 11 – Out of Session Work

As stated in the tutor notes, it is likely that the flowchart will take several sessions and as such the out of session work will be to continue to expand the flowchart a little.

If the offender really grasps the concept and proves adept at completing the flowchart, simply ask them to complete a new flowchart for a different situation for their out of session work.

Exercise 11 – Review

Name at least one thing that has been learned from this exercise.

Additional Notes:

Exercise 12 – The Round Up

Category of exercise: Self Awareness

Tutor Notes

Although this session is the final session in the sequence, it reuses Session 1 as a way to summarise what has been taught in previous meetings by rounding up as many of the learning points as possible.

Step 1: Draw the *My Trigger Triangle* on the worksheet provided or ask the offender to draw it.

Step 2: Ask what this triangle represents and why it is important, as part of a general discussion.

Tip: If the offender struggles with this, ask leading questions such as 'What have the previous exercises focused on?', 'How does each point of the *Trigger Triangle* inform the next?' and 'Why do we look at thoughts and feelings as well as behaviour?'

Step 3: Try to draw out from the client: *If we can think about the consequences of our behaviour, then we can change our feelings and subsequent behaviour in any given situation.* Also try to elicit why this fits with victim empathy – in that if we care that our behaviour may make a new victim, then we can try to change the behaviour to prevent this.

Step 4: Ask the client what they feel they have learned from the previous sessions. The tutor should again record this on the worksheet.

Exercise 12 – The Worksheet

Draw the *My Trigger Triangle* in the space below:

What have you learned from the trigger triangle?

Exercise 12 – Review

Write down what you have learned from the exercises in this workbook.

1.

2.

3.

4.

5.

6.

7.

8.

9.

10.

11.

12.

The Questionnaire again

Step 1: Provide the questionnaire for the offender to complete.

Step 2: Review their answers from this questionnaire and question or challenge any obviously anti-social answers.

Step 3: Total the score, this time with the offender.

Step 4: With the offender, compare the scores from this and the previous questionnaire as well as looking at any changes in answers

Tip: Don't forget to use MI skills and be specific in praise where awareness has increased, as evidenced through a change in answer.

The Questionnaire

Please circle the answer that best describes how you feel about your offence and explain further where required.

Answer on a scale of 1 to 5, where 5 is you agree strongly with the statement, and 1 is where you totally disagree.

1. I am the victim of my offence.

1   2   3   4   5

If you have circled 3 or above, please explain your answer here:

2. My offence has not affected anyone else.

1   2   3   4   5

If you have circled 3 or above, please explain your answer here:

3. The offence was the victim's fault.

1   2   3   4   5

If you have circled 3 or above, please explain your answer here:

4. I did not think about how my offence would impact on others before I acted.

1   2   3   4   5

If you have circled 3 or above, please explain your answer here:

5. My offence has not impacted on the victim's family.

1   2   3   4   5

If you have circled 3 or above, please explain your answer here:

```



```

6. My offence has not affected the community I live in.

1   2   3   4   5

If you have circled 3 or above, please explain your answer here:

```



```

7. Looking at the scale of offending in this country, my offence is relatively minor and unimportant.

1   2   3   4   5

If you have circled 3 or above, please explain your answer here:

8. There are other people involved in my offence who need to take some responsibility for my offending.

1   2   3   4   5

If you have circled 3 or above, please explain your answer here:

139

9. There is a lot of fuss being made about the victim, instead of considering my feelings.

1   2   3   4   5

If you have circled 3 or above, please explain your answer here:

10. The consequences of my offence are limited to the short term.

1   2   3   4   5

If you have circled 3 or above, please explain your answer here:

11. Paedophiles who are murdered because of their offending behaviour are not victims.

1   2   3   4   5

If you have circled 3 or above, please explain your answer here:

12. If the victim had reacted differently once the offence had started, events may have been different at the end.

1   2   3   4   5

If you have circled 3 or above, please explain your answer here:

13. It is difficult to think about a 'victim' as a victim, when that victim is a large organisation, a shop or the community.

1   2   3   4   5

If you have circled 3 or above, please explain your answer here:

14. I agree that whilst my actual offence is illegal, in my circumstances there should be more understanding and less punishment.

1   2   3   4   5

If you have circled 3 or above, please explain your answer here:

15. There was no victim, only potential victims.

1   2   3   4   5

If you have circled 3 or above, please explain your answer here:

```



```

16. The cost to the community of offending, in terms of money or emotions, is minimal.

1   2   3   4   5

If you have circled 3 or above, please explain your answer here:

```



```

17. I believe victims should have to attend crime awareness courses so that they can prevent themselves from being victims again in the future.

1   2   3   4   5

If you have circled 3 or above, please explain your answer here:

```
┌─────────────────────────────────────────────┐
│                                               │
│                                               │
│                                               │
│                                               │
└─────────────────────────────────────────────┘
```

18. This focus on victims and victim awareness is not going to help me.

1   2   3   4   5

If you have circled 3 or above, please explain your answer here:

```
┌─────────────────────────────────────────────┐
│                                               │
│                                               │
│                                               │
│                                               │
└─────────────────────────────────────────────┘
```

19. There is only a 'long term' impact to my offending because professionals won't stop talking about the offence.

1   2   3   4   5

If you have circled 3 or above, please explain your answer here:

```



```

20. Even if I knew just before my offence/at the time of my offence, that my behaviour would create a victim, I do not think that I would have behaved any differently.

1   2   3   4   5

If you have circled 3 or above, please explain your answer here:

```



```

```

```
Please add up your scores and put the total here:

CPSIA information can be obtained
at www.ICGtesting.com
Printed in the USA
BVHW020727090723
666954BV00011B/1114

9 781909 125186